The New Revised

HELPING YOURSELF
WITH
SELECTED PRAYERS

ORIGINAL PUBLICATIONS
22 East Mall
Plainview, New York 11803

ISBN: 0-942272-01-3

TABLE OF CONTENTS

INTRODUCTION
By Henri Gamache

Prayer is the master key. A key must fit one door of a house, but when it fits all doors it may well claim to be the master key. Such and no less a key is prayer to all earthly problems.

Tennyson said, "pray for my soul, more things are wrought by prayer than this world dreams of". In a single sentence, the poet has summed up the power of prayer... far better than your author could ever hope to do... in many pages. Here is the crystalization, the very essence of the result of thoughtful prayer.

Prayer is an art and requires practice. The first requirement is a controlled imagination. Just to vainly repeat a set prayer is foreign to any true prayer. Praying is more than mere words; it must come from deep within one; from the very soul. Prayer must be felt just as one feels coolness or warmth; just as one is affected by other senses, such as taste, smell, hearing, etc.

The exercise of Prayer requires tranquillity and peace of mind. Some people surround prayer with ceremony to lend an air of solemnity. It is most important that one feel the presence and nearness of God. One can pray as well in an open field as one can within the shadows of a great cathedral.

The essence of prayer is faith. However, faith must be permeated with understanding to be given the active quality which it does not possess when standing alone. What does this mean? Simply that a prayer which lies hidden between the covers of a book - no matter how beautifully written; no matter how promising in its message; no matter how urgently repeated will never do anyone any good unless it is given the Motive Power to send it to its goal.

Where does this Motive Power come from and whence is its goal? The Motive Power must come from within you and its movement must be directed toward God from whom all earthly favors come.

Anyone can make their prayers come true. This is as sure as the rise of tomorrow's sun. A prayer will not come true simply by mouthing words, however; a lot depends upon your mental attitude, your faith and sincerity of your praying. It also depends upon your ability and wisdom to ask for things within reason - NOT for a million dollars the following afternoon; not for recovery from a long standing illness just over night; not for some impossible request which perhaps would do you more harm than good.

THE LAW OF PRAYER

Prayer is governed by laws just as surely as any other process of life. At first thought this seems a sacrilege yet sober reflection and analysis will make one realize that this is so.

Let me explain in simple language how the law of prayer works. For generations, since some most ancient time, the existence of electricity was known. It was known that by rubbing a stick of ebony with a piece of silk (friction) electricity could be produced. Yet *it was not known* that electricity could *produce friction!*

The existence of sound was known. One was heard to speak or sing. One heard music of an orchestra, the singing of birds, the other sounds of nature but no one dreamed that these same sounds could be reproduced mechanically by means of a phonograph.

In nature all *force* is *reversible*. Heat can produce mechanical motion, mechanical motion can produce heat. *Electricity* can produce magnetism, magnetism can produce electrical currents, such currents can reproduce the voice and other sounds.

Here then, is the crux of the matter: Cause and effect; energy and matter, action and reaction. It is of importance to remember these things to understand them for by understanding them one can **see *the direction from which their prayers may be answered.***

If, for example you knew how you would feel if your prayer were to be answered, and if you could realize, consciously, just how you could awaken such a feeling in yourself, you would have travelled a long way toward learning how to make your dreams come true.

How many times have you perhaps read in some metaphysical work the thought, "Believe that you already possess that for which you pray". To many this seems premature, yet it is based upon the law of Inverse Transformation.

If your *realized prayer* produces in you a *definite feeling* or *state of consciousness*, than by *inverse process,* that particular feeling or state of consciousness *must produce your realized prayer.*

Because all transformation of force is reversible, *you should always assume the feeling of your unfilled wish.* You should awaken within yourself the feeling that you are and have that which heretofore you desired to be and to possess. The easiest way to accomplish this is to contemplate the joy that would be yours if your objective were an accomplished fact. Act and move and live and feel that your wish is already realized.

"Faith is the substance of things hoped for, the evidence of thins not seen". Assume the feeling of your fulfilled wish and continue feeling that it is fulfilled until that which you feel comes to realization.

In Mark 11:24 we find "What things soever ye desire, when ye pray, believe that ye have received them, and ye shall have them". If this has seemed too deep for comprehension before reading, this, certainly must now have become clear.

IMAGINATION AND PRAYER

Imagination is the beginning of creation. You must imagine what you desire and you must believe it to be true. Your every dream could be realized if you were self-disciplined enough to believe it. People are what *you* choose to make them; *You,* yourself, must look at a man with different eyes before he will change objectively for you. Two men looked from a prison window; one saw the mud and muck of the earth; the other saw the stars. Do not judge by appearances; see a man as *you* desire him to be.

Before going on to the prayers which follow in this book, the foregoing pages should be studied thoroughly and an attempt made to try to awaken the *feeling* as described therein.

In order to accomplish this, make some simple wish, some simple luxury that you have wanted. Do not ask for a big thing, an impossible thing, ask for some little thing that you have wanted, but felt that you just couldn't afford to get at the moment... and that you have

3

been putting off getting because you didn't have the extra cash. Perhaps it may be something that you could afford to get if you wanted to but you feel that the money might be better spent some other way. Try to awaken in yourself how you would feel if you had that certain something. Try to sense the satisfaction and the sense of elation you would have if you did have that something. Try to act and think and feel and live just as if you already had that thing. Imagine how you would show it to your friends; how you would rejoice in it. Pray conciously and sincerely and fervently for it... and it will come to you.

When you first determine what this thing is to be, you may not even know where the money is coming from. But it will come if you believe that it will come and you maintain that faith!

In publishing this book Original Publications is responding to a demand for an English version of many popular prayers formerly available only in Spanish.

Helping Yourself with Selected Prayers is a collection of prayers most often requested by the English reading public. Provided are the English translations for over one hundred prayers of various religious beliefs, spiritualism, and superstition. Many are what might simply be called folk prayers.

These prayers are not given to be followed verbatim. They are given merely as examples of the kind of thinking that should be followed in attaining a given objective. The reader is warned that words without acts will go for naught. These examples which follow are just that, samples. Make up your own prayers and affirmations as you go along. Learn to pray consciously and vigorously and sincerely and honestly. Try to feel the force of your praying. True prayer can come only from within yourself.

✟✟ *PRAYER TO SAINT ANNE* ✟✟

It is believed, however unconfirmed, that during a time of lament and prayer St. Anne the wife of St. Joachim was visited by an angel and despite being well beyond her child bearing years miraculously became pregnant and later gave birth to the Blessed Virgin Mary. Those who pray to Saint Anne may seek spiritual healing, blessings, insurance against poverty, and tranquility. **JULY 26**

✟✟ Oh, Holy and glorious Saint Anne. Faithful wife of Saint Joachim. For your humility and faith in the laws of God which were given to Moses, you were chosen in the fruit of your live to be the purist and most holy mother of all women.

Oh, glorious Saint, mother of Mary, grandmother of Jesus Christ. I call to you and beg you, have my wishes answered by God, to the satisfaction of you and your holy husband. I am in a situation of debts and miseries, overwhelmed by uncertainty and tribulation. Amen. ✟✟

(You must start and end this prayer by invoking the Holy Trinity. Repeat three times and make your wish.)

✝✝ PRAYER TO ✝✝ SAINT ANTHONY OF PADUA

During the 13th century Saint Anthony of Padua preached throughout Italy with distinct power and eloquence. His sermons denounced corruption, wrongdoing and injustice. He became reknowned as a miracle worker and a patron of the poor and oppressed. He is depicted in art with the Infant Jesus on his arm because of an episode in which a visitor described witnessing this. Saint Anthony of Padua is the Patron Saint of Lovers and Marriages. He is often called upon for Special requests, forgiveness of greed, improvement of memory and the return of lost articles. **JUNE 13**

✝✝ *Oh wonderful Saint Anthony, glorious on account of the fame of thy miracles, and through the condescension of Jesus in coming in the form of a little child to rest in thy arms, obtain for me of His bounty the grace which I ardently desire from the depths of my heart. Thou who was so loving towards miserable sinners, regard not the unworthiness of those who pray to thee, but the glory of God that it may be once again magnified by this request which I now make to you. Amen.* ✝✝

✝✝ PRAYER TO SAINT ALEJO ✝✝

✝✝ *Oh, my glorious Saint Alejo, you who have the power to take away all evil that surrounds the Lord, I ask you to take my enemies far away from me. Take me away from the devils, take me away from the liars, and also from the sinners, and finally, take those who would harm away from me. Put me so far from those evil ones that they will never see me. Take away all those who have evil thoughts and wish harm to me. Bring me closer to the Lord so that in His Divine Grace I will be covered with goodness. So be it.* ✝✝

✠✠ PRAYER TO ✠✠
SAINT ANTHONY

At 20 years of age, after the death of his parents and the inheritance of their vast wealth, Anthony came upon a passage in scripture imploring that in order for one to become perfect he must relinquish all of his wealth to the poor. In the year 285 Anthony seeking the strictest seclusion retired to a fort on Mt. Pispir where he remained for twenty years, he had no contact with any other human, his food was thrown to him over a wall of the fort. Upon his emergence he founded the first Christian monastery. During his life Saint Anthony was challenged with constant bouts of temptation by evil and struggles with the devil. He disciplined himself with prayer, penance and fasting. People of all backgrounds and circumstance throughout Egypt sought Anthony's advice. Those who pray to Saint Anthony petition for miracles. **JANUARY 17**

✠✠ Oh, sweetest Savior of mine. What a good time this is to receive your mercy and forgiveness, now that the Church is celebrating in the sacred name of Saint Anthony, and being in his arms and filling them with love, what could you deny us being your humble servant, our intermediary?

Let the Holy Fountain of your mercies be shed upon us. Let the doors of Heaven be opened by you, Great Saint Anthony, so that we may receive your grace.

Turn your glorious face to us, devotees of Saint Anthony, who, trusting in your help, promise to reform our lives, confess our sins, obey your sacred laws, and give infinite love to the Blessed Mary. Filling us with hope and love will give us the strength of your Blessed Heart to defeat the spirit of darkness. So Divine Father, as we hear the melodies that the Church intones today in honor of Saint Anthony, raise your almighty hand and forgive and bless us in our needs. Amen. ✠✠

✟✟ UNFAILING PRAYER TO ✟✟
SAINT ANTHONY

✟✟ Oh holy St. Anthony, gentlest of Saints, your love for God and charity for his creatures, made you worthy, when on earth, to possess miraculous powers.

Miracles waited on your word, which you were ever ready to speak for those in trouble or anxiety. Encouraged by this thought, I implore of you to obtain for me (request).

The answer to my prayer may require a miracle, even so, you are the Saint of Miracles.

Oh gentle and loving Saint Anthony, whose heart was ever full of human sympathy, whisper my petition into the ears of the sweet Infant Jesus, who loved to be folded in your arms; and the gratitude of my heart will ever be yours. ✟✟

✟✟ PRAYER TO ✟✟
SAINT APARICIO

✟✟ I implore, Saint Aparicio, as the Infant Jesus appeared, with your power and patience help me find all that I have lost. Let it appear as I invoke your glorious name. As I walk through dangerous paths, my Guardian Angel shall appear in my presence. Intercede for me, and at the time my lips pronounce these three words, "It must appear," Saint Aparicio will lead me to whatever was lost.

Nothing shall stand in the way of what I wish to find. I shall never ask for the impossible, only that which is justly and rightly mine. As you found and gave the Lost Infant to his legitimate mother, I want you to do the same for what is mine. Amen. ✟✟

✝✝ PRAYER TO ✝✝
THE HOLY INFANT OF ATOCHA

In the city of Atocha in Spain during Moor occupation a small child appeared at a prison where Christians were held. The child had with him a pail of water and a basket of bread. All the prisoners there were nourished by the bread and water yet the basket and pail remained full. The moors were astonished and the word quickly spread through Spain that the Christ child had taken compassion on the prisoners and had come to alleviate their suffering. This is how the belief in the Holy Infant of Atocha was born.

✝✝ Holy Infant of Atocha, general protector of all mankind, strength of the invalid, and divine doctor of all illness. Powerful Infant, I salute you and offer you three Our Fathers, Hail Marys, and Glory Be to God.

In your memory on this day I ask you to grant me my petition. Purist Infant of Atocha, with my heart I ask and pray that I will not be disappointed. I am sure you will be with me when I find my peace and join you in the heavens of Bethlehem. Amen. ✝✝

Make your petition now. Say three Our Fathers, Hail Mary, and three Glory Be to God.

✝✝ AN ACT OF CONSECRATION TO ✝✝
OUR LADY OF THE MIRACULOUS MEDAL

✝✝ Virgin Mother of God, Mary Immaculate, we dedicate and consecrate ourselves to thee under the title of Our Lady of the Miraculous Medal. May this medal be for each one of us a sure sign of thy affection for us, and a constant reminder of our duties toward thee. Ever while wearing it, may we be blessed by thy loving protection and preserved in the Grace of thy Son. Oh most powerful Virgin, Mother of our Savior, keep us close to thee every moment of our lives. Obtain for us, thy children, the grace of a happy death; so that, in union with thee, we may enjoy the bliss of heaven forever. Amen. ✝✝

✝✝ PRAYER TO THE 12 AUXILIARY SAINTS ✝✝

✝✝ *Humble, compassionate Auxiliary Saints. Counselors and ministers of this world under the authority of our Eternal Father, Son, and Holy Spirit. Send us a reflection of your heavenly light as you sent your grace to that wicked man who gave bread that turned into coal to the poor. As you did to Ciprian and Justina for their wickedness and witchcraft. As you did Magdalena for her freedom and Saint Dionisio for his compassion to our God on the Cross. To Veronica for wiping our Lord's face when he was on the holy cross. Cleanse the doors of my home and my soul, and let no evil stand in my path. Saint Barbara, defeat with your holy sword my enemies. Saint Michael, guard and revoke our enemy Lucifer. Dominate the evil tongue of _____ as the Virgin Mary dominated the wild beast. Guard my health. If I look for work, let me find it. If I should lose something, let Saint Anthony help me find it. I beg that whatever I desire, I will soon have, Father, Son and Holy Spirit. Amen. ✝✝*

✝✝ GREAT ENCHANTMENT IN HONOR OF ✝✝ THE SELECTED BARON OF THE CEMETERY

✝✝ *Baron, Selected of the Cemetery, three times I call your holy name. With the help of the powerful strength of Cain, you will give me your three selected spirits, so man or woman born may not do an act of treachery against me, and no injustice will condemn me. Let all evil and perverse ideas that _____ may have against me be revoked. Make them come humiliated and repenting with all their hearts to me, by the order of the Baron of the Cemetery. Amen.*

Assist me in life, and console me in death, with Thy most amiable presence, and present me to the Most August Trinity as Thy devoted servant and child; that I may eternally bless and praise Thee in Heaven. Amen. ✝✝

✝✝ *PRAYER TO SAINT BARBARA* ✝✝

Legend says that St. Barbara was the beautiful daughter of a wealthy nobleman named Dioscorus, who had her shut up in a tower to discourage the attentions of her numerous suitors. Upon discovering that she had become a Christian, he attempted to have her killed, but she was miraculously transported out of his reach. He then denounced her to the authorities who submitted her to torture. When she refused to renounce Jesus her father was ordered to kill her. This he did by beheading her with his own sword. All at once a bolt of lightning fell from heaven and struck him, turning him to ashes. This is the source of St. Barbara's power over thunder and lightning. The virgin martyr is the patron saint of gunners, miners and firemen. Her special symbol is a tower. **DECEMBER 4**

✝✝ Magnificent and eternal God, we admire your Saints, especially the glorious Virgin and the Martyr Saint Barbara. We give thanks for those who were worthy of your intercession and were freed from all evil, helping them in their hour of need, not permitting them to die without receiving the Holy Sacraments, and granting them and assuring them that their petitions had been heard. I beg everything by the merits of the dear Saint Barbara.

Give me strength to resist temptations and to know my faults. And so to be worthy of that sacred and Holy Virgin, especially in my hour of death, fortified with the Holy Sacraments and by them and the intercession of Saint Barbara, happy in your company with you and with your glory, where you live and reign in Heaven. Amen. ✝✝

✠✠ *PRAYER TO* ✠✠
SAINT BARBARA LUCUMI

✠✠ *Glorious Saint Barbara, my Black Virgin! You who were born on this earth and, for your gifts of power and goodness, carried to heaven; I admire your greatness and I have confidence that you can free me and protect me from fire, witchcraft, and sudden death, and that you can Protect my house and all that surrounds it from evil influences, envy, jealousy, and faithlessness.*

With your holy power, conquer victoriously. With your cloak protect me; with your hands bless me; with the holy power that God gave you, and your enchanted spirit, conquer without turning back, and always be firm in your decision to protect those who are faithful and plead for your protection.

Free me, my mother, of all evil temptations, and do not abandon or forget me.

This request comes sincerely from my heart! ✠✠

(Pray three Hail Mary and three Creeds.)

✠✠ *My most holy mother! Thank you for having heard my petition. May god increase your charms and those who believe in you will become more faithful, and await your charity. Amen.* ✠✠

✠✠ *PRAYER TO SAINT BLAISE* ✠✠

✠✠ *Oh, Lightened soul of our Lord, Holy Martyr, helped along by God. You found delight and security and abundance in the desert. Alone you created numerous miracles, converted by the faith of Jesus Christ. Those with faith and devotion call upon you. They call upon Him who made heaven and earth a glorious place. Rid us of sins and eternal torment.* ✠✠

✞✞ *PRAYER TO SAINT CHRISTOPHER* ✞✞

There are no dates about either the birth or death of Saint Christopher. The story that circulates in the West is that he was a man of gigantic stature who wanted to serve the mightiest of masters. He lived alone by a ford where he earned a living by passing travelers on his shoulders across the waters. One day a child appeared and asked to be carried across. Half way through the ford the child became so heavy that the giant was barely able to finish the crossing. When St. Christopher complained to the child about his unusual weight, the child told him that the heaviness he felt was the weight of the world that he was carrying on his shoulders. The child then revealed himself as Jesus Christ, whereupon St. Christopher fell down on his knees and declared that he had finally found the master he was seeking. He is the patron of travelers and of the city of Havana. **JULY 25**

✞✞ Grant to those who invoke you, glorious Martyr Saint Christopher, allow them to be preserved from epidemics, and earthquakes, from the rages of storms, fires, and floods. Protect us with your intercession during life from the calamities that Providence may hold for us. During death free us from convictions, assisting us during the last hour, that we may reach eternal good will. Amen. ✞✞

✝✝ PRAYER TO ✝✝
SAINT CHRIST OF GOOD HEALTH

✝✝ Oh sweet Jesus on the cross, only son of the Eternal Father and of the immaculate Virgin Mary! Like a poor man I come to you who are merciful. Like a child that is ill I come to you, the true doctor and only giver of health, our Lord Jesus. Do not allow me Lord, to leave your presence without remedy. Grant me that which I humbly ask by your adored Heart, and by your loving Mother. Do not consider my faults which would obligate you to abandon me, but attend to my merits which prove me to be deserving. Show me the way with your superior merits and care; I want to be more deserving. From now on and forever I will be grateful for your mercy, and I shall praise you eternally. Amen ✝✝

✝✝ SAINT CIPRIAN AND SAINT JUSTINA ✝✝

✝✝ Glorious and holy Saint Ciprian and your loyal companion Saint Justina, from your infancy, you were deserving of the Lord's holy blessing. Accustomed to seeing the heavenly perfections of Jesus and Mary in their holy temple, reach for me merciful son and mother, so that my soul will find no peace if not in your continuing greatness. Put an end to all the evil habits of this world, and find mercy in your kindness. Grant me merciful Saint Ciprian this favor, and especially grant those for whom I am saying this prayer. Amen. ✝✝

✝✝ PRAYER TO SAINT CIRO ✝✝

✝✝ Miraculous Doctor, marvelous and glorious Martyr Saint Ciro. Glorious Protector, I have complete confidence in your power, and I am positive you will receive this petition. I call upon you. I shall try to imitate your excellent virtues and pray I will be deserving of your help in guiding my way to find perfection. In your company I give repeated thanks to the Trinity for enriching my divine spirit. Amen. ✝✝

✝✝ *PRAYER TO* ✝✝
SAINT COSMAS AND SAINT DAMIAN

Cosmas and Damian were brothers and doctors, who lived in Syria during the 3rd century. They were widely known and called upon for their medical skill and reknowned for never charging a fee. They were arrested during the persecution of the Christians, tortured and then beheaded for their faith. Cosmas and Damian are the Patron Saints of Physicians. The devout seek assistance in the relief of ailments and for spiritual guidance. **SEPTEMBER 27**

✝✝ Holy and admired Martyrs Cosmas and Damian. Full of admirable glories and favors by the merciful divinity, I worship your kindness and pray to see you for all eternity. Crowned with glory and praise by our Lord, you are honored with many graces. I beg you to intercede with the Divine Majesty by presenting my plea, especially this prayer, so that the Lord will help me with my spiritual needs and the illness that I have. Amen. ✝✝

✞✞ *CARIDAD DEL COBRE* ✞✞

The traditional story of this Virgin says that around the year 1620 two Indians and a Black Slave went to the Bay of Nipe near the mining province of Cobre to look for salt. As they were rowing in their canoe, they noticed a strange object among the waves. As they approached, they saw that what had attracted their attention was an image of the Virgin Mary that was floating on a piece of wood. The image was approximately 15 inches long, carved in wood. In one arm the Virgin held the Infant Jesus and on the other a cross of gold. The legend at her feet read: Yo Soy La Virgen de La Caridad (I am the Virgin of Charity). The three men picked up the image and brought it to Santiago where a small chapel was built in her honor. In 1916 she was declared patron of Cuba. The many miracles of La Caridad are counted in the millions. **SEPT. 8**

✞✞ Oh, unique spirit, without beginning or end, ever present, ever powerful, in whose ocean of life I am but a drop, let me feel the presence of your power, let me know more clearly what you are and what I mean to you. Make the consciousness of your spiritual reality penetrate my whole being and occupy all the parts of my soul.

May your spiritual power which is in my soul penetrate the body of this other being in my own body who wants to be cured, infusing it with health, vigor, & vitality, so that it can become a better temple of the Holy Spirit. Give this body the peace, strength, and life that belong to you by virtue of your being. This I ask of you, oh ever present spirit, because I am your son and because of your promise of eternal knowledge. Amen. ✞✞

✝✝ *PRAYER TO SAINT CLARE* ✝✝

Inspired by a sermon by Saint Francis in the early 13th century, St. Clare ran away from home on Palm Sunday to live her life for the church. St. Francis placed her in the Benedictine convent. In 1215 Francis placed her in charge of the convent at St. Damiano where she remained superior for forty years. Clare founded the Poor Clares an order of nuns who spoke only when necessary and vowed poverty. This Order grew throughout Italy and spread to France and Germany. During her life Clare was credited with many miracles and relied upon for consultation by cardinals, bishops and Popes. St. Clare is summoned for understanding and protection from evils. **AUGUST 11**

> ✝✝ *Glorious Virgin and distinguished mother Saint Clare, clearest mirror of holiness and purity, light of all the virtues. For all the favors which the Divine Husband granted you in such abundance, and by the special right of having made your soul the throne of his infinite greatness, reach out for us with your unbounded piety, to cleanse our souls of stains and faults. We also ask you for peace and tranquility of the church, so that the unity of faith, and the holiness of customs will always be conserved and that we will become immune to the efforts of our enemies. And if it is for the greater glory of God and the good of my spirit, you, as Mother and Protector, present my wishes in Divine dispatch, and with your infinite kindness I will reach for your greater honor and glory. Amen.* ✝✝

✞✞ *PRAYER TO* ✞✞
SAINT ELIJAH

✞✞ *Glorious Father and prophet of God, Elijah. Great caretaker of Honor and Founder of the Order of Mary of Mount Carmel. From the crest of the mountain you came with a spirit of prophecy. And a small cloud coming up from the sea descended in abundant rainfall over the narrow fields of Israel, as a symbol of the graces which Mary had poured over the world with her holy scapular.*

Being fed with the Holy Eucharist, may I walk through the desert of this life without fainting, as you walked, nourished by bread baked under ashes, to the Mountain, shunning the sinful Jezebel. Teach me to avoid the deceit of this world and the cleverness of the Devil so that by imitating your devotion for the glory of God, someday I may be at your side, singing the praises of God and of his holy Mother, whom I desire to see and love eternally. So be it. Amen. ✞✞

✞✞ *PRAYER TO* ✞✞
ST. ELIJAH OF MOUNT CARMEL - REVOCATION

✞✞ Powerful Saint Elijah of Mount Carmel, holy and virtuous man of God, guide of the mortals who are without a path. Kneeling before you, I beg that you help me rid my home of all evil spirits which may reside in it. I also beg, Siant Elijah, as you tamed the enemy which tried to harm the person you protect, I may defeat all those who wish to harm me. Lend me your sword to overcome all the harm which may have been done and prevent any harm in the future.

I beg you my Saint, do not abandon me in the hour of danger. Help me in this hour to find peace in my home. Take an interest in my improvement, and do not allow any of my enemies to harm me.

I offer to light a candle for fifteen days and on the last day an oil lamp of pure olive oil so that you may clean my home. Amen. ✞✞

Say one Our father, Hail Mary and Glory Be to God.

✞✞ *SAINT ELENA* ✞✞
OF JERUSALEM

✞✞ Glorious Saint Elena, daughter of the Queen of Jerusalem. You went to Jerusalem and brought three nails. One you consecrated, and on Tuesday threw it into the sea. The other you gave to your brother Ciprian so that he would win battles and wars. The one you have left in your holy hands, I ask for, but only as a loan to penetrate the senses of _____ so he will not forget me, to penetrate his brain and heart so he shall have me close to him. Saint Elena, the nail which I ask for is to keep me in his thoughts and make him come to me. Don't let him lie in a bed nor speak with another woman. I ask that he never forgets me for another woman. Jesus, bring him to

*me. Saint Barbara, don't allow _____ to forget me.
Saint Anthony, see that _____ does as he promised
me. Saint John the Baptist, who was Holy before birth,
grant me what I ask. Have _____ carry out his
promise for the Holy Spirit. Saint Michael, step on him,
Saint Ciprian, hear me and give me what I ask. Saint
Elena stir his heart and bring him to me. Amen. ✝✝*

✝✝ *PRAYER TO* ✝✝
GLORIOUS ELEGUA

Elegua is one of the most revered and powerful messengers to god in the Yoruba and Santeria religions. Elegua's function is to test and try out the human spirit and help human beings along their evolutionary paths. One of his main concerns is the enforcement of the divine will and the punishment of those who choose to ignore cosmic laws.

Santeria is a Spanish term that means the confluence of Saints and their worship. During the time when African slaves, worshippers of Yoruba, were brought to Cuba they were forbidden the practice of their religion by their Spanish masters. In order to continue their religious observances safely the slaves opted to identify their deities with some of the Catholic Saints worshipped by the Spaniards. There are at least 21 saints with which Elegua has been identified, Saint Anthony of Padua, the Holy Infant of Atocha and the Lonely Spirit (Anima Sola) to name a few.

✝✝ To You, Lord of the roads, glorious warrior immortal Prince, I raise this humble supplication.

Keep evil away from my home, keep my home safe from evil in my absence, and when I am present, when I am awake, and when I am sleeping, and accept my daily prayer to the Great Olofi asking His eternal blessings for you. Amen. ✝✝

✟✟ *PRAYER TO* ✟✟ *SAINT EXPEDITUS*

✟✟ Oh glorious Martyr and protecting Saint of ours, Saint Expeditus, having faith in your great merits and above all in the precious blood of Jesus Christ. We humbly beg of you to reach out to us and send us from God the necessary virtues to make us good and pious. And by studying and exercising your virtues, we can practice them and follow your example here in life so that we can deserve the merits of glory. Amen. ✟✟

✟✟ *PRAYER OF* ✟✟ *SAINT FRANCIS OF ASSISI*

✟✟ Lord, make me an instrument of your peace. Where there is hatred, let me sow love; where there is injury, pardon; where there is doubt, faith; where there is despair, hope; where there is darkness light and where there is sadness, joy.

Oh Divine Master, grant that I may not so much seek to be consoled, as to console; to be understood as to understand; to be loved, as to love.

For it is in giving that we receive; it is in pardoning that we are pardoned; it is in dying that we are born to eternal life. ✟✟

✝✝ *GOD LOVES YOU* ✝✝

✝✝ *Dear God above, thou art mighty over all the universe and all therein. Thou art ever present and all understanding.*

As mighty as thou art, dear Lord, I feel your gaze upon me. I hear your message of abundant love and kindness. Thou art my Father, you guide and protect me. For this I am eternally grateful.

Please, dear God, guide me always to have this trust and devotion in Thee. When I am confused or distressed, in times of fear or pain, remind me of your presence and assist me.

Help me, Almighty, to comprehend your commandments and to live by them at all times, for if I do so I will be blessed forever with good health and happiness, and my family will feel your guidance and enjoy your blessings forever. Amen. ✝✝

✝✝ *PRAYER TO* ✝✝
SAINT GABRIEL

Saint Gabriel was sent by God to Daniel to explain his vision and prophecy,. he proclaimed the birth of Christ to Mary, and foretold the birth of John the Baptist to his father Zechariah. **SEPTEMBER 29**

✝✝ *Glorious Prince of the Court of Heaven and most excellent Saint Gabriel, first minister of God, friend of Jesus Christ, and favored by the Holy Mother. Defender of the church and lawyer of man. You favor our devotions and help me to love and serve you. Grant me what I desire and ask for with this prayer, for the honor, glory and fulfillment of my soul. Amen.* ✝✝

✝✝ *PRAYER TO SAINT GEORGE* ✝✝

Legend has George a Christian knight as a hero who saved a village from a ferocious dragon who terrorized their lives daily. To keep the dragon satisfied the people offered sheep for its consumption. When there were no more sheep, human sacrifice became necessary. George rode through town on the day that a princess was to be sacrificed, it is told that Saint George lifted his lance, motioned the sign of the cross and with a single blow killed the beast. As reward the King offered George half his kingdom. George declined, requesting of the King only that he keep the faith and have pity on the poor. Upon his departure 20,000 townspeople converted to Christianity. **APRIL 23**

> ✝✝ *Powerful Lord, example of the humble, you defended us from the vices of the demon with your lance, to bring us to Heaven. Through your humbleness, glorious Martyr Saint George we humbly ask for your intercession and victory over dangers which afflict us. We will achieve a haven of happiness after our trials and tribulations. We shall pass safely through life, and then praise you in Heaven. Amen.* ✝✝

✝✝ *PRAYER TO THE THREE VIRTUES*, ✝✝
FAITH, HOPE AND CHARITY

✝✝ *Oh, all powerful God, Father of all that exists. Never let me lose faith, so I may continue to love and adore you. Oh Christ, son of God, example of gentleness and humility, instill in me the necessary energy so that Hope may be the comfortable balm to help me complete the destiny of my life.*

Oh, Holy Mother of Christ, Queen of the Heavens, full of purity and virtue. You whose heart is full of Charity. You help all who are in need. Dignify me to carry in my heart the reflection of your radiant soul so that I can also give to all those who are in need.

All these virtues of Faith, Hope, and Charity be reverently exercised, I beg you to grant what I ask for my good, and that I obtain my wish. I shall practice these virtues until the hour of my death.   Amen. ✝✝

✝✝ *PRAYER TO* ✝✝
THE HOLY TRINITY

✝✝ *May the Son guide me, the Father keep me, the Holy Spirit be with me. May I be blessed with grace by the Virgin. With her holy cloth may I be covered. With the Lord's robe may I be wrapped, so that I may not be hurt, jailed, or killed. God be with me and I with him.*

May the powerful God give me fortitude and be with me. The consecration of the Holy Trinity be with me.

Jesus Christ, Savior of the World, remove the evil of my enemies. Remove all evil that would keep me from the road of goodness with God our Father, with God the Son, and with God the Holy Spirit.   Amen. ✝✝

✠✠ PRAYER TO SAINT GERARD OF MAYE

Saint Gerard dedicated his life to helping others. He di earnings to his mother, to the poor, and to the church. He l ___ame a lay brother in 1748 in Italy for the Congregation of the Most Holy Redeemer. He became known for his supernatural abilities of prophecy, mind reading, healing , and being able to appear in two places at the same time. It was believed that he had the power to influence animals and nature. He is the patron of childbirth. **OCTOBER 16**

✠✠ Oh glorious Saint. You who suffered so from adversity and endured so much pain. You were persecuted, and slandered, yet endured so admirably, maintaining sound peace of mind. Reach out to me the spirit of fortitude in all adversities of my life.

How might I attain the virtue of patience. The smallest work frightens me. The smallest obstacles hurt and anger me. I must come to realize that it is only through the path of tribulations that Heaven is reached. Guide me through this journey of life, Saint Gerard. Give me the strength to embrace willingly the crosses that God sends me so that afterwards I will deserve to be with God in Heaven. So be it. Amen. ✠✠

✠✠ PRAYER TO ✠✠
THE GUARDIAN ANGEL

✠✠ Protecting spirit who watches over me always, you who have this mission, now for the joy of doing good and for progress and purification of your spirit, save me, for during the night my spirit goes to meet the unknown. Take me to where my loved ones and my friends are and those who want to help me. Help me with all the problems of my life. Oh, that the revelations I should put into practice would be held fast in my imagination.

Give me strength in my contemplation of nature and raise my spirit above the new struggles that have made my hopes vanish. Amen. ✠✠

✝✝ *PRAYER TO THE GREAT POWER* ✝✝

✝✝ Protect me, Great Power of God. Let the strength of Jesus' faith be with me. Let purification be with me. Let the ecclesiastical court of the Most Holy Trinity crush the courage of my enemies so that they do not harm me, my children, or my benefactors. Jesus Christ, Redeemer, you conquered the world from the cross. Let your death conquer my enemies. Amen. ✝✝

After this prayer, say the prayer to Saint Michael. It is to be repeated three times beginning with a Creed and ending with another Creed.

✝✝ *PRAYER TO* ✝✝
HIGH JOHN THE CONQUEROR

✝✝ Hi John the Conqueror, Hi John of the Street. As you dared to enter the Holy Temple of Jerusalem and put out the candle of the Sacred Altar. Enter always the five thoughts of _____ and do not let him think of anyone. Let him think only of me and no one else. Let him not sit in a chair, nor lie in a bed, nor have a moment of tranquility until he comes defeated to my feet. Amen. ✝✝

(Use an oil lamp for 9 days)

26

✟✟ HOLY VIRGIN OF GUADALUPE ✟✟

✟✟ Remember, merciful Virgin Mary of Guadalupe, with your heavenly presence in the mountain of Tepeyac, promising your loving clemency and compassion to those who love you and ask for your help in their lives, offering to hear our pleas, cleanse our tears, and give us hope. Never has it been said by those that reach out to you, that you have not given your protection to those who need it. Never have you abandoned us. With this confidence we come to you, Virgin Mary, Mother of God.

Though we are sinners, we prostrate ourselves before your image praying that you will grant your merciful promises. We pray that nothing nor anyone will harm us. May we not have any sickness, fear, pain, accident, nor any suffering. As an admired image you have stayed with us. You, who are our Mother, our health and life, we need nothing more. Do not deny us. Oh, Holy Mother of God, listen to us with compassion and grant our pleas. Amen. ✟✟

✟✟ PRAYER TO THE INDIAN ✟✟

✟✟ Oh, Great Chief, faithful Indian Spirit. In the name of the Father, the Son, and the Holy Ghost, I, a faithful believer in your power, ask you in this moment, to help me. Oh, Great Spirit, you know my problems. Help me with your power, and guide me with your holy and divine protection.

Oh, Great Indian Spirit, I ask you in the name of Jesus, offer me your protection, and with your axe break the chains that my enemies bind me with spiritually and in all money matters.

With the poison of your arrows destroy the evil thoughts against me. With your eyes see that no one does me harm in any way. Amen. ✟✟

✝✝ *PRAYER TO* ✝✝
THE INFANT JESUS OF PRAGUE
(Powerful Novena in Urgent Need)

✝✝   *Oh Jesus, who hast said, "Ask and you shall receive, seek and you shall find, knock and it shall be opened by you," through the intercession of Mary, Thy most Holy Mother, I knock, I seek, I ask that my prayer be granted. Amen.*
(Make your request now.)

Oh Jesus, who hast said, "All that you ask of the Father in my name, He will grant you," through the intercession of Mary, Thy most Holy Mother, I humbly and urgently ask Thy Father in Thy Name that my prayer be granted. Amen.
(Make your request now.)

Oh, Jesus, who hast said, "Heaven and Earth shall pass away, but my word shall not pass," through the intercession of Mary, Thy most holy Mother, I feel confident that my prayer will be granted. Amen. ✝✝
(Make your request now.)

In cases of great urgency, a novena of hours may be made instead of days. The prayers should be repeated at the same time every hour for nine hours.

✝✝ *GLORIA* ✝✝

✝✝ *Glory be to the Father, and to the Son, and to the Holy Ghost, now and forever. As it was in the beginning, let it be now forever and ever. Amen.* ✝✝

✞✞ AN OFFERING A MOTHER MAKES ✞✞ FOR HER CHILDREN TO THE INFANT JESUS OF PRAGUE

✞✞ Adored Infant Jesus of Prague, adored son of Mary Virgin and Immaculate Mother, I wish to honor the angels and saints in heaven and the just hearts of those on earth. I am but a poor creature without merit and with many sins. You who know the value of a child to a mother's heart, accept the gift of love and honor which I offer, as I dedicate this prayer.

I give you my child, he is yours. Keep him from all danger of body and soul. Bless his heart so he may always be pure. Bless his eyes so they will not be fascinated by the temptations of vanity. Bless his inclinations so he will never stray from virtue. Bless his soul, his power, and senses. Divine Infant, you have promised favor to those who honor you. I entrust to you what I love most in this world, my son . . . my son, dear Jesus, son of the Virgin.

What shall be of my son tomorrow? Will he love his parents? Will he be good, or will he get lost?

How much does a mother criticize? You know, my God, you who reads the intimate soul. The heart of a mother rests in you, Divine Infant Jesus of Prague. Amen. ✞✞

✞✞ PRAYER TO LA MADAMA ✞✞

✞✞ Oh Holy Spirit, I implore your sublime influence for my protection. By the virtue of God I ask you to help me with my needs in this life and smooth my way. Oh spirit of the "Madama" give me courage. Use your influence so that no one may harm me. From your treasure chest give me some wealth to help me in my needs. I ask this with faith. Amen. ✞✞

Use *Original* "Madama" perfume for more strength.

✝✝ *PRAYER TO* ✝✝
THE NINE SOULS OF LIMA

✝✝ This candle which I am lighting, in nine days shall be consumed by the souls that I invoke. They will protect me with all their power. All that I ask will be granted. Our Father, Hail Mary and Glory.

Anguished Souls, move the heart of _____ so his heart will be full of love for me. All that he has, he will give to me. Our Father, Hail Mary and Glory.

Souls who killed their bodies treacherously, inspire the heart of _____ that all the grudges and evil will go away. May he not think of anything but my affections with humility and all his desires be of me and of making me happy. Our Father, Hail Mary and Glory.

Souls who died captivated by love, look at the grief which I am suffering. Let his grudge become affection and in an instant turn to happiness. Our Father, Hail Mary, and Glory.

Souls who died doing good for mankind and in return are seeing God's face, inspire in the heart of my opponents peace. Take away their bad will, and with their own mouths, confess the errors of their ways. Let them ask for my forgiveness, and may I become victorious in this great enterprise which I am about to begin. Our Father, Hail Mary and Glory.

Souls which died innocent of crime, for your grief without fault free me from all treachery. Watch over me so that my enemies and opponents cannot do me any harm. Any power they have will be taken away. Our Father, Hail Mary and Glory.

Souls who died in their beds, look at the grief that I am suffering. Let my enemies and opponents have no tranquility or rest. Let them come to give satisfaction, and without knowing it, they shall have growing love for me with ties so strong that only death can separate us. Our Father, Hail Mary and Glory. Amen. ✝✝

✟✟ 15 MINUTES IN THE COMPANY OF ✟✟ JESUS SACRAMENTARIAN

✟✟ Holy Sacramentarian, King of the Divine Justice, here I come my father to beg for my health and that of my family and those who surround me. Also grant me, my father, the best of luck in your reign. Come visit me, until the bad luck that I have and the people who wish us harm are driven far away from us.

Holy Sacramentarian, Divine Majesty, you who gave us our being, I come to beg and ask for good luck in my business so that I may be free of necessities that today I suffer, promising always to favor my neighbor in his needs and bring peace to my home. ✟✟

Now say one creed. This Prayer is said at 12:00 or 3:00 in the afternoon on Thursday or Friday.

✟✟ Bleeding Jesus Christ, scarred and full of blood, throw your arms over me and my enemies Do not allow them to go against me. ✟✟

Say one creed to the Powerful God.

✟✟ Victorious Jesus Christ, who on the cross over-came everything, for the death you suffered I beg you to help me. Admonish all to carry this holy blessing, be-cause it is known through experience to be marvelous against demons, temptations, rays, odors, problems of the heart, and enemies. It is powerful against storms, fires, pains of labor, fevers, sudden deaths, and all harm and illness. May the Lord have mercy and give you peace. May the Lord give you his blessing. Amen. ✟✟

✝✝ SACRED HEART OF JESUS ✝✝

✝✝ Lord Jesus Christ, who said, "Ask and you shall receive, seek and you shall find," look at me, prostrate at your divine feet with vivid faith. Full of confidence in your promises, dictated by your Sacred Heart and pronounced by your adorable lips. I implore you to hear my prayer.

To whom can I go, if not you, whose heart is a fountain of inexhaustible graces and merits? Where shall I look, if not in the treasure which contains the riches of your clemency and generosity? Where can I call, if not at the door which leads us to God?

To you Oh Divine Heart of Jesus I do go. In you I find consolence to my afflictions, protection when I am being persecuted,strength when I am dejected. I firmly believe my Jesus, that you can pour over me the grace which I implore even if a miracle is necessary. I only have to desire it and my wish will be granted. I recognize my Jesus, that I am not deserving of your favors, yet there is no motive to discourage me. You are the God of compassion, and you will not refuse a repenting and humiliated heart which comes to you with confidence. I implore your compassionate heart to find in my miseries and faults a justified motive to grant me my petition.

Oh Sacred Heart of Jesus, whatever your decision may be, I will never stop adoring, praising, loving and serving you all my life. Lord, accept this act of perfect submission. I sincerely desire to obey and honor you. Amen. ✝✝

✝✝ HAIL MARY ✝✝

✝✝ Hail Mary full of grace, the Lord is with thee, blessed art thou among women, and blessed is the fruit of thy womb, Jesus.

Holy Mary, Mother of God, pray for us sinners, now and at the hour of our death. Amen. ✝✝

✝✝ PRAYER FOR SAINT ROSE OF JERICO ✝✝

✝✝ Divine Rose of Jerico: For the blessings received from our Lord Jesus Christ, for the virtues that you hold and the power considered, help me overcome the difficulties of life, give me health, strength, happiness, comfort and peace in my home, success in business, talent at work, to earn money to cover the necessities for my home and family.

Divine Rose of Jerico: All this I ask for the virtues you hold in love to Jesus Christ and his divine mercy. Amen. ✝✝

Say three "Our Father".

Instructions:

The rose is to be put in a saucer of water at 9:00 or 3:00 o'clock on Tuesday or Friday. Leave it in water for three consecutive days, remove the flower the same hour it was put in and pray with all your religious faith.

Faith is what saves, and if you do not have faith nothing can reach the virtues of this plant.

This plant that is completely dry, recovers life and its natural green color when contacted with water.

Use the remaining water to sprinkle the corners of all the rooms and at the front door of your home, to erase bad influence, and bring PEACE, POWER and ABUNDANCE to your home.

✝✝ PRAYER TO OUR LADY ✝✝

✝✝ My Queen! My Mother! I give thee all myself, and show my devotion to thee. I consecrate to thee, my eyes, my ears, my mouth, my heart, my entire self. Wherefore, Oh loving mother, as I am thine own, keep me, defend me, as thy property and posession. Amen. ✝✝

✟✟ SAINT JOHN THE BAPTIST ✟✟

Saint John the Baptist was the son of Zachary and Elizabeth. Zachary had been told by the angel Gabriel that his wife would give birth despite her old age. John lived as a hermit in Judea until the age of thirty. In 27 A.D. he began to preach throughout Jordan warning "Repent, for the Kingdom of Heaven is at hand". Among his many followers was Jesus Christ who came to John for Baptism. Upon recognizing Christ as the Messiah, John is quoted (Matt 3:14) "It is I who need baptism from you". He preached that the masses follow Christ *"the lamb of God"*. John the Baptist is the Patron Saint of Evangelists and is prayed to for good luck. **JUNE 24**

> ✟✟ *Glorious Saint John the Baptist, predecessor of my Lord Jesus Christ, beautiful star of the best sun, trumpet of Heaven, voice of the eternal Word, you are the oldest of the saints, lieutenant of the King of Glory and son of the grace of nature. For all these reasons you are the most powerful in Heaven. Grant me the favor I ask, if it is beneficial to my salvation. If it is not, I shall resign myself with abundant grace, and, becoming a friend to God, I will be assured of eternal happiness in Heaven. Amen.* ✟✟

Say one Our Father and one Hail Mary.

✟✟ OUR LADY OF MERCY ✟✟
(Our Lady of Mercedes)
SEPT. 24

> ✟✟ *Holy Virgin Mary of Mercy, Mother of God and for the majestic quality of dignity which is expressed with respect by the angels and man. Today as one of your children, I confess, since my childhood I have had you as my mother, lawyer and patron. Since that time you have given me your grace and have answered my pleas for protection. With your power, help those who during life were faithful and lead them to eternal happiness in heaven after death. Amen.* ✟✟

✞✞ *PRAYER TO ST. JOSEPH THE WORKER* ✞✞

In the New Testament in Luke 4:22, Joseph is mentioned as the father of Jesus. He was married to, but not living with, Mary at the time she became pregnant. This befuddled Joseph to the degree that he sought to divorce Mary, at this point he was visited by an angel who informed Joseph that her pregnancy was by "the Holy Spirit".

Not much else is known of Joseph other than that he was a hard working and honest man who descended from the House of David. Joseph is the Patron Saint of All Workers, Patron of the Universal Church and Patron of Social Justice. Pope Leo XIII declared him as the model father, his assistance is sought for family unity. **MARCH 19**

> ✞✞ *Glorious Saint Joseph, patron of all who are devoted to toil, obtain for me the grace to toil in the spirit of penance, in order thereby to attone for my many sins; to toil conscientiously, putting devotion to duty before my own inclinations; to labor with thankfulness and joy, deeming it an honor to employ and to develop, by my labor, the gifts I have received from Almighty God; to work with order, peace, moderation, and patience, without ever shrinking from weariness or difficulties. To work above all with a pure intention and with detachment from self, having always before my eyes the hour of death and the accounting which I must then render of time ill-spent, of talents unemployed, of good undone, and of my empty pride of success, which is so fatal to the work of God.*
>
> *All for Jesus, all for Mary, all in imitation of thee, Oh patriarch Joseph! This shall be my motto in life and death. Amen.* ✞✞

✝✝ *PRAYER TO* ✝✝
SAINT JOSEPH

✝✝ Noble Joseph, head of the Sacred Family, executioner of the infalable and designator of knowledge and infinite mercy. Father of Jesus and happy husband of Mary. How I rejoice in seeing you elevated to high dignity, and adored with heroic virtues. For the sweet hugs and kisses which you gave the Infant jesus, I beg you admit me from this point in the happy number of your brotherhood.

Protect the virgins, tutor of the virginity of Mary. Reach out to us the grace to conserve without blemish, the purity of body and soul. Take pity on the poor and the sick. For the sweat and grief which you suffered in order to save the Creator and Savior of the Universe. Give us the bodily nourishment, make us have patience in the work of this life and to treasure the infinite riches for eternity.

Guide all parents. Oh happy Patriarch, make the fathers and mothers the image of your virtue and perfection. Make them models of mercy with their children. Protect the priest and religious institutes and imitating your life, fill the obligation of their ministry with perfection.

Fill our lives with blessings. Don't abandon us powerful lawyer, those who are in need. You had the happiness of dying in the arms of Jesus and Mary. Reach out to us, so that we may die repenting for our sins and pronouncing with fierce affections the sweet names of Jesus, Mary and Joseph. Amen. ✝✝

✝✝ *PRAYER TO* ✝✝
SAINT JUDE THADDEUS

Saint Jude also known as Thaddeus, was the brother of St. James the Less. He preached in Mesopotamia in the first century with his fellow apostle Simon. Jude is believed to have written the Book of Jude in the New Testament. He is widely called upon by those who find themselves in dire circumstance. He is the Patron Saint of Impossible Cases. **OCTOBER 28**

✝✝ I believe, Oh glorious apostle St. Jude, that you are in Heaven at the favor of Jesus Christ, contemplating divine peace, possessing God, being absorbed in a thousand delights that constitute your eternal happiness.

You returned the graces of Jesus with constant loyalty, and you loved Him with all your heart.

Your devotion made you fly to instill in the heart of the multitudes, the productive seed of truth of the Protector of the despaired.

In payment for so much courage and for your most worthy works, sinners spilled your blood with insane cruelty.

Give me the grace to repent for my sins, to live with His friendship, to imitate your example, and to die fulfilling my duties as a Christian.

Grant it to me. If what I ask from god does not oppose my eternal salvation, give it to me, as I entrust you with veneration and faith. Amen. ✝✝

Say three Our Fathers, three Hail Marys, and glory to the Father.

✝✝ *PRAYER TO SAINT LAZARUS* ✝✝

There is not much known about Saint Lazarus. He was the brother of Martha and Mary, and a close friend of Jesus. It is believed that Jesus raised Lazarus from the dead. Four days after he was placed in a tomb, Lazarus emerged without showing any sign of impurity or imperfection. **DECEMBER 17**

> ✝✝ *Oh Blessed and Glorious St. Lazarus of Betony, protector and supporter of Martha and Maria. I call on you, oh, beloved and always vivid spirit of grace with the same faith that Jesus called to you at the door of your tomb, from which you exited after being buried for four consecutive days, without any sign of impurity or imperfection. Oh, holy spirit I call upon you with the same faith that God had in you to consider and grant what I ask for in this prayer. Amen.* ✝✝

✝✝ *PRAYER TO THE* ✝✝ *GLORIOUS SAINT LUIS BELTRAN*

> ✝✝ *Creature of God, I cure you, enchant and bless you in the name of the Father, Son, and Holy Spirit, three persons and only one true essence. Our Virgin Mary, Our Lady, who conceived without original sin, and for the glorious Saint Gertrude, your loved and gifted wife, Eleven Thousand Virgins, Holy Joseph, Saint Roque, and Saint Sebastian and for all the Saints of your heavenly court.*

> *For so high and holy mysteries, which I believe are true, I beg your Divine Majesty, that your Holy Mother and lawyer will intercede for me. Please free and heal the afflicted creature of this illness, pain, or accident. I beg you Lord for your mercy. Divine Majesty, do not permit any accident or harm to come to me. Grant me health so that I may serve you and comply with your holy will. Amen.* ✝✝

✟✟ *PRAYER TO SAINT LUCY* ✟✟
(Special Lawyer of the Eyes)

Lucy was born to noble parents in Sicily around the year 280. She dedicated her life to God and hoped to use her family's wealth to help the poor. She refused marriage after three years of engagement to a young nobleman, the source of their discord was Lucy's generosity. In response he denounced to the Emperor Diocletian who persecuted her as a Christian. Lucy was condemned to a brothel, but when the guards physically tried to remove her from the court they were unable budge her. Oxen were brought in to drag her, but she could not be dragged. Finally, the Emperor ordered that she be burned, but even the flames could not harm her. She was finally put to her death by the sword of an executioner when he stabbed through her throat.

Lucy is known as the Special Lawyer of the Eyes and is prayed to by people who have vision problems perhaps because of her name which means light. She is also called upon to conquer temptation and in quests for love. **DECEMBER 13**

> ✟✟ *Oh! Saint of God, blessed Saint Lucy, who is placed at His right hand. As against the foe we stand, pray for us Saint Lucy and help me in this plea. (State your purpose) I give this situation to you humbly and with confidence in the knowledge that, with your prayers and intercession in this matter, justice, goodness and mercy will prevail.* ✟✟

Note: To reach highest grace make your petition and say three Our Fathers and three Hail Marys.

✝✝ *PRAYER TO SAINT MARCOS OF LEON* ✝✝

✝✝ *Saint Marcus of Leon, who avoided the disgrace of the dragon, tame the hearts, evil sentiments, evil thoughts and unhappiness against me. Peace, Peace, Christ, Christ, Dominum Nostrum. Saint John, your friends come. Let them come.*

Peace, Peace, Christ, Christ, Dominum Nostrum. Detain them as Our Lord Jesus Christ was detained at the hour of his death. Your enemies are fierce as a lion, but they shall be tamed by Saint John and Siant Marcos of Leon, and all shall come to your feet as they came to the foot of the tree and the Cross.

Peace, Peace, Christ, Christ, Dominum Nostrum. Amen. ✝✝

✝✝ PRAYER TO THE VIRGIN MARY ✝

✝✝ Holy Lady of mine, who has suffered more in ti
life than our Lord Jesus? Who has been battered by a
guish and unhappiness? Who has suffered more pain?
the pain and torment which your forgiving heart we
through. Not only did they serve to be more similar in ti
suffering of your son and increase your crowns, but also
sympathize with those who suffer, helping those submerge
in the gulf of misery and calamity. We would drown if n
raising our eyes to you, we are saved. I am in the prese
hour afflicted. I have nothing to wait for, nor see any plac
in which I can rest, and I have no other refuge. There is r
other star to look at but you, in whose sweet arms I go
and whose faithful patronage I trust. I believe that thos
who humbly ask your help, will find a way out of their mis
ery. I beg you to help me in my time of need. Amen. ✝✝

✝✝ MARY & THE LODESTONE PRAYER ✝

✝✝ Mary, mineral and enchanted Lodestone, you tha
with the Samaritan have been to whom name and beauty
has given, luck and good fortune will bring to me. Lodestone you have been in the past, Lodestone you will be in
the future, and as a guardian you will be in my company. I
ask of you gold for my treasure, silver for my home and
copper for the poor, and as you have been a luminary for
the Holy Virgin, so I want you to be for my humble home.
Guardian of my household and of my body, I want it to be
prosperous and happy and that my lucky star should guide
me and enlighten my path.

Lend me your magic powers. Lend me your luck. I wish
to have wealth and power in order to defeat my enemies. I
wish that my lucky star guides me and enlightens my path.
Peace on earth, goodwill toward men. Amen. ✝✝

✝✝ *MOTHER OF PERPETUAL HELP* ✝✝

✝✝ *Refuge of SInners, Mother of Mercy, Holy Virgin Mary, see me humbly repentent before you imploring your blessing. Confident of your goodness, I pray to reach your Divine Son. Receive Mother, my heart and all aspirations of my soul, desires, and thoughts. With your powerful help and guidance, prepare my spirit so my offering will be worthy of you. Amen.* ✝✝

✝✝ *Mother of Perpetual Help, powerful Virgin Mary, give me your light for knowledge. Excite my heart so I may know your excellence, and knowing you, love and praise you. Purify my heart against evil, and let me love thy Son and you, Holy Mother, in this life, and rejoice eternally in Heaven. Amen.* ✝✝

✝✝ *Oh, Mother of Perpetual Help, grant that I may ever invoke Thy most powerful name which is the safeguard of the living and the salvation of the dying. Oh, Purest Mary, Oh Sweetest Mary, let Thy name henceforth be ever on my lips. Delay not, Oh Blessed Lady, to help me whenever I call on Thee, for in all my needs, in all my temptations I shall never cease to call on thee, ever repeating Thy sacred name Mary, Mary. Oh what consolation, what sweetness, what confidence, what emotions fill my soul when I utter Thy sacred name, or even only think of Thee. I thank god for having given Thee, for my good, so sweet, so powerful, so lovely a name. Let my love for Thee prompt me ever to hail Thee, Mother of Perpetual Help. Amen.* ✝✝

✠✠ *PRAYER TO* ✠✠
SAINT MARTHA

During the first century Martha and her brother and sister, Lazarus and Mary lived in a small village outside of Jerusalem. Jesus was a friend of the family and frequently a house guest. It was an annoyance for Martha that her sister Mary did not help around their home, and sat for hours listening to the preachings of Jesus. Christ's response to Martha was that each person chose their own place in life and that she should not make judgements about the path that others choose.

Martha moved to France where she spread the word of Jesus in the Rhone Valley. A mythical tale recounts that her village was threatened by a fire-breathing dragon whose arose from a river. Martha defeated the dragon by spraying it with holy water. **JULY 29**

✠✠ *Oh, holiest Saint Martha, you who walked through the Mountains and were able to tame the Serpent, take care of me. I humbly ask of you to protect me from my enemies, make my soul pure, and give me eternal salvation. Amen.* ✠✠

✠✠ *Oh, Virgin Saint Martha, Dominator of the serpent. You who saved a child from sure death when a serpent was coiled around him, in this way, dear Saint Martha through the intercession of Saint Cipriano, I ask that you free me of all malice and punish anyone who wishes me harm by allowing the serpent to dominate him, curling up around his body until he repents and gets on his knees to ask for forgiveness.*

This way I surrender my faith to Saint Winslow and Saint Cipriano so that my husband (or lover, or boyfriend) attends to me only. Amen. ✠✠

✝✝ PRAYER TO SAINT MARTHA ✝✝
(Dominator)

✝✝ Holy Virgin Martha, for the oil which you will consume today, for the oil which nourishes this lamp, for the wick which burns away all impurities, I dedicate this lamp so that you may relieve me of my miseries and help me to overcome all difficulties. As you dominated the beast at your feet, give me health and work so that I may provide for my needs.

My mother, grant me that _____ may not live in peace until he comes to stand at my feet. This way my Mother, for the love of God, grant my petition and eliminate my miseries. Amen. ✝✝

✝✝ Holy Virgin Martha, who entered the mountain and tied up the beast with your ribbons, I beg you to tie up and dominate _____ .

Saint Martha, let him not sit in a chair nor lie in a bed until he is at my feet. Holy Martha, hear me, help me for the love of God. Amen. ✝✝

✝✝ 15 MINUTES WITH SAINT MARTHA ✝✝

✝✝ Saint Martha, take me into your protection and guide me. I offer myself completely to your mercy and grace. I offer this candle in your honor for the happiness our Savior received in your home. I plead with you to intercede for me and my family so that all our daily needs will be provided, and may we always have love of God in our hearts. I also ask you to obtain the infinite mercy of God in granting me this great favor. (Here ask your favor.)

Help me to overcome my difficulties as you dominated the dragon at your feet. I ask this favor in the glory of God. Amen. ✝✝

Say one Our Father and one Hail Mary.

✟✟ THE NINE TUESDAYS ✟✟ OF SAINT MARTHA

✟✟ Holy Martha, I surrender to your guidance and protection, honoring your wishes. To prove my act of contrition and actions of grace I shall offer this light in your honor every Tuesday.

Console me in my sorrow. Bring happiness to my home in the name of our Holy Savior, Jesus Christ. Provide me and all my family with our daily needs.

I implore you with your infinite mercy to grant the great favor I ask. (Make your petition here.)

Today I ask you, as you dominated the Dragon at your feet, defeat all my enemies. Amen. ✟✟

✟✟ PRAYER TO ✟✟ OUR LADY OF THE HELPLESS

✟✟ Sovereign Queen, how it pleases my soul to be near your powerful greatness. Even though I am not a deserving subject, for so many times have I deserved the indignation of your son, my Savior, for my sins and faults, please take me under your guidance and protection. You are my anchor of faith in the dangers and misfortunes of life. Lend me your grace so that from now on, with all my heart, I will render you devotion. I shall be attentive and punctual, admitting the divine laws that guide the destiny of eternal life.

I _____ , promise God and the Holy Cross that you shall follow behind me, as the living behind the Cross and the dead behind the light, saying three Our Fathers to the Intranquil Spirit to grant me what I have asked. ✟✟

✝✝ *PRAYER TO THE MOST HOLY JUDGE* ✝✝

✝✝ *Oh, Just and Holy Judge, blessed son of the Virgin Mary, let my body be calm and my blood be washed so that wherever I may go, the hands of my Lord Jesus Christ be in front of me. That of St. Andrew before and after me. Saint Peter's in the back and the middle. Those of the Virgin Mary, that my enemies may come and go with eyes but without seeing me, with arms but without hurting me, and that justice may not apprehend me. That my body be covered with the cloth that covered Jesus Christ's body, that I may not be hurt, or dead, or incarcerated.*

Oh, Virgin Mary, this prayer I say for good or bad that my enemies may hold against me. If any sentence be in this day against me, let it be revoked by the blessings of the Father, Son and Holy Ghost. Amen. ✝✝

✞✞ *PRAYER TO* ✞✞
SAINT MARTIN

At age 15 Martin was sent to serve in the Roman Army. By age 23 he had discovered Jesus and although still a soldier, lived his life like a monk, he refused further service pleading "I am a soldier of Christ and it is not lawful for me to fight". He worked tirelessly throughout his life to spread Christian belief and convert pagans, including his own parents. It is believed that Saint Martin's first religious experience arose as a result of a meeting with a beggar on a brutally cold night during his military tour. Martin cut his cloak in half and offered it to the man. That night Martin was visited in his dreams by Christ clad in his half cloak "Martin has covered me this day" said Jesus.

Saint Martin is the Patron Saint of Conscientious Objectors. He is prayed to by those suffering impure thoughts. **NOVEMBER 3**

> ✞✞ By the sign of the Holy Cross, free us from our enemies in the name of the father, the Son, and the Holy Ghost. Amen. ✞✞

> ✞✞ Oh, merciful God, who told us of Saint Martin, a perfect model of humility and charity. Who, without looking at his own condition, faithfully he served until glorified in God's Kingdom with the Angels.

> And you Saint Martin, who lived only for God, and for your good works. You who were so understanding to all unfortunately poor people. Piously attending those who admired your virtues and who recognized your power. They praised you to God.

> Make us feel the effects of your great charity, bring us closer to God, who faithfully rewarded your merits with eternal glory. Amen. ✞✞

✞✞ *REVOCATION OF* ✞✞
SAINT MICHAEL ARCHANGEL

St. Michael along with St. Gabriel and St. Raphael are the three archangels mentioned in the bible. St. Michael's purpose is to fight against all evils and protect the souls of man against the devil. He is often pictured with a sword fighting a winged dragon, this relates to his mention in the New Testament. St. Michael and his angels battle the dragon and his followers and throw them from heaven. **SEPT. 29**

✞✞ Saint Michael Archangel, as you are the person in charge of all the works in the world, I implore you at this solemn hour and day, seize this time so that you will see the light, candle, and work. Come sorcery and corruption and revoke yourselves in my body. The flesh and blood of my enemy should treat me well.

Let my enemies suffer as Jesus suffered on the Cross, bitterness, torment, kicks and slaps.

Let him go into a desolate world. Let him take the three falls that Jesus took until he comes to my home asking pardon for his sins. The stars in Heaven bear witness to my pleas. So be it. Amen. ✞✞

48

✟✟ *PRAYER TO ST. MICHAEL* ✟✟

✟✟ Saint Michael the Archangel, defend us in the day of battle and be our safeguard against the wickedness and snares of the devil. We humbly pray, by the power of God, cast into hell, Satan and all other evil spirits, who prowl through the world, seeking the ruin of souls. Amen. ✟✟

✟✟ *PRAYER TO THE* ✟✟
GLORIOUS ARCHANGEL SAINT MICHAEL

✟✟ Glorious Lord Saint Michael Archangel, especially favored by God Our Lord. Selected and destined to guard and protect the Holy Catholic Church, and great goodness and salvation of the souls. For the divine mercy, we have great happiness in living in your holy society. In your sacred beliefs and faith we desire to live and die. Humbly, we beg that you look after our country which is so Catholic and has served the church of Christ which you defend and guide. We beg you, who are captain of the armies, to defend it against its enemies. As an angel of peace, you reduce it to harmony and unity, and as the highest justice of God. Judge of the souls, you shall conserve the justice and equality. Our Lord selected you to throw the rebels out of heaven, and to you we come so we may reduce the rebels of this earth and calm its alterations. You stopped the Angels republic, so prepare and conserve our republic. You cleaned the heaven of sinners, free our country of them also.

Our Lord gave you to us, as a universal patron of all the faithful and to you we come as a single protector, and we expect from you a particular protection. We beg you conserve your providence in all purity of faith and do not permit to enter heresy or seeds of evil doctrine, but conserve and communicate true faith as you have with other nations. To have peace between all nations and to obey God and all divine things. This we beg for the love which you have for Jesus Christ, heaven and the elevation of the church Amen. ✟✟

✝✝ SPELL OF SAINT MICHAEL ARCHANGEL ✝✝

✝✝ I _____ offer the 14 Enchantments of our Lord Jesus Christ and the powerful sword of Saint Michael Archangel to enchant _____ who wishes to fight with me. He shall not fight with me because he will be prevented by the 14 Enchantments of Our Lord Jesus Christ and the powerful sword of Saint Michael Archangel. With his knives he shall not cut me, with his gun he shall not shoot me, and with his tongue he shall not cause me harm.

I _____ offer the 14 Enchantments of Our Lord Jesus Christ and the powerful sword of Saint Michael Archangel that if I should be arrested by the law, they shall never send me to jail.

One, in body and soul I salute you. Two, with two eyes I see you. On three I tie you up. I shall break your heart, and you shall come before me humiliated.

I _____ offer the 14 Enchantments of our Lord and the powerful sword of Saint Michael to enchant all my enemies. Amen. ✝✝

✝✝ OUR LADY OF MONSERRATE ✝✝

✝✝ Holy Mother of love, life, refuge, and hope of mine. You, who being worshipped in Monserrate by the holy image, helped the poor, the invalids, orphans, and the unhappy out of their misery.

Grant me, Mother of the chosen, refuge for sinners and the unhappy, so that I, being a sinner, may triumph over the ignorance of my duties. Help me care efficiently with prayers and good conduct to help the young who are going in the direction of sin and teach them to follow and love God.

You can, Protector and hope of mine. This is what I hope to gain, that after being blessed with the Infant Jesus here on earth, I may see Him and praise Him forever in Heaven. Amen. ✝✝

✝✝ PRAYER TO ✝✝
THE MOST POWERFUL HAND

✝✝ Thou who has suffered, reach out thy hand to me with a great blessing. Thy pierced hand with thy saintly fingers inspires my humble prayers. Jesus said, "Ask and it shall be given to you." Through thy most precious blood I seek, and I ask that my prayers may be heard and granted.

I carry a likeness of your pierced hand with me always as a loving symbol of your great kindness. And I call on the graces necessary for peace and happiness. Grant me this request. Amen. ✝✝

✝✝ PRAYER TO SAINT PANCRACIO ✝✝

✝✝ Glorious Saint Pancracio, special lawyer for health and work. Intercede before the Lord for me so that I may have your help in the favor I desire, if it is to be in the glory of God and to good of my soul. Amen. ✝✝

✝✝ You know Lord, it is my obligation to ask for your help in my necessities. If my petition is just Lord, send your messengers to help me and direct me in the manner which I should use to gain favor. Amen. ✝✝

✟✟ *PRAYER TO THE APOSTLE SAINT PETER* ✟✟

St. Peter's given name was Simon. He worked as a fisherman with his brother Andrew. Andrew introduced Peter to Jesus and they both became followers. Jesus called upon them to recruit others. Jesus gave Simon the Aramaic name Cephas equivalent of the Greek Peter (the Rock). Jesus named St. Peter one of his apostles and declared him "the Rock on which I will build my Church". He bestowed upon St. Peter "the keys to the kingdom of Heaven" and the powers of "binding and loosing". Peter is mentioned in the gospel more than any of the other apostles and was present for many of Christ's miracles. Those faithful call upoin St. Peter for strength and forgiveness of their sins. **JUNE 29**

✟✟ Glorious King of the Apostles to whom our Lord Jesus Christ spoke first after his glorious and wonderful resurrection. We beg you to grant us the grace that the Lord designated you to give us, and for the intimate thoughts of your conscience. To think about us poor people and forgive us our faults, Glorious Saint Peter and grant us this grace so that we can purify our souls by means of true pain and cleanse ourselves of everything that has offended you. Grant that by the help of this inter- cession, we may be released from the bonds of our sins. Amen. ✟✟

✟✟ PRAYER TO ✟✟
SAINT RAPHAEL

Saint Raphael is one of the seven archangels, and one of only three along with Gabriel and Michael identified by name in the scriptures. Raphael was sent by Jesus to accompany Tobias, a blind and ill man across the desert to meet and wed Sara whose seven previous bridegrooms had been slain by the devil on the night of their wedding. St. Raphael chased the evil spirit from Sara and cured Tobias of his blindness and ills enabling the two to enjoy marriage. The name Raphel means "God has healed" he was given the power by Jesus to "move the waters" by which the ill are cured. Raphael is the Patron Saint of travelers and safe journeys. Those who call upon St. Raphael seek assistance with all of their ills; physical, mental and spiritual. **SEPTEMBER 29**

✟✟ *My Lord Saint Rafael, I come with happiness to you, so that you may help me resolve all my problems in less than 21 days. Also, guide me as you did with the young Tobias.*

Faithful companion and custodian. Destined by the Divine Providence so that you may guide, protect, and be my defender, may you never leave my side. I shall thank you for your faithfulness and love every instant that you are with me. As I sleep, you watch over me. When I am sad, you comfort me, and when I am hungry, you feed me. Saint Rafael, you keep all dangers away from me and guide me towards goodness. I would be burning in Hell if you had not helped me to reconcile with God. I plead with you not to desert me. Help me to prosper and keep from danger. Help me to conquer temptations so that I may find in my life and soul the grace of Jesus, Mary and Joseph, Joaquin, and Ann. Amen. ✟✟

(Make your petition now.)

✝✝ PRAYER TO SAINT RAYMOND ✝✝

✝✝ Glorious Saint Raymond, protector of the angels who come to this world, guardian of souls, I leave myself in your divine and perfect mercy. Kneeling at your feet, I ask for your protection and help in this painful peril which is getting near. I come to you as a humble servant at your feet, begging for your vigil and charity to help my soul and the soul of the innocent angel which is to arrive in this land of sinners. I ask for forgiveness. If I, unhappy and humble sinner, have ever offended you, I beg for your forgiveness. Amen. ✝✝

✝✝ PRAYER TO ✝✝
THE HOLY VIRGIN OF REGLA

St. Augustine, an African bishop who lived from 360 to 436 A.D. was visited during his youth by an angel who told him to carve the image of the Virgin on a piece of wood and to place her on his altar. The image that St. Augustine carved became known as the Virgin of Regla. It was brought across stormy waters to Spain by one of Saint Augustine's disciples named Ciprian. The Virgin is known as Our Lady of Regla because Saint Augustine and his followers lived by very strict disciplines which the saint called his "rule", which translates as *regla* in Spanish. The Virgin of Regla is the patron of all sailors and men of the sea. **SEPT. 7**

✝✝ Holy and sweet Virgin Mary, mother of God, daughter of the Highest King and mistress of the angels. Mother of our Creator, Queen of Mercy, receive me under your protection. Help me, for I need your help. In your temples all have found help for their problems. Sailors in the worst storms have called on you Virgin Regla, and you have led them to safety. Those being persecuted by their enemies have been saved by their devotion to you. Even those on their death beds have been healed by your powers. Queen of Heaven, we implore you and your holy Son for health, comfort, and strength to serve and worship you. We ask for your help in our necessities of life. Especially help those who say this prayer. Amen. ✝✝

✝✝ PRAYER TO SAINT ROQUE ✝✝

✝✝ Merciful confessor of Christ, glorious Saint Roque, another David of the law, defender of the gentle and righteous heart. The new Tobias, with tender affection for the poor and for those who are constant in their faith. What else shall I prove to Heaven besides patience and fortitude? How happy it makes me to know in this world of ambition you appear so humble, giving your blessings to the poor and begging for bread as a pilgrim. As if nothing was wrong, not the scars or pains which you suffered, nor the hunger nor the abandonment in which you found yourself, until having no other resource or guidance but the bread you received from Heaven, you continued on your way and did not rebel. Oh you have suffered for the pride, ambition, and sexuality of man. It is not strange that you are visited with favors and heavenly grace while I am punished by the divine justice for the bad habits and sins I have committed. You who liberated Rome and many other cities from devastation, liberate me also, and liberate the world which puts all its confidence in you. Fulfill in us sweet promise from Heaven which was written on a mysterious slate that appeared over your glorious body. Amen. ✝✝

✝✝ PRAYER TO ✝✝
THE HOLY VIRGIN OF THE ROSARY

✝✝ Remember forgiving Virgin Mary, that you have never failed to hear those who come to you imploring your help. You protect them and would never abandon them. Encouraged by this confidence, I come to you Virgin Mother of all Virgins. I beg you crying and trembling like a sinner that I am, suffering in your presence, Oh Mother of the Divine Trinity do not ignore my pleas. Hear them and take them kindly. Amen. ✝✝

Our Holy Father Pius IX grants 300 days of indulgence for every time that we pray the first prayer. Those who pray it once daily were granted worldly indulgence each month. For confessing and receiving communion, visit one church and pray there. It is enough to visit the High Altar.

✟✟ *SAINT SYLVESTER* ✟✟

Sylvester was a Roman who was elected bishop of Rome to succeed Saint Miltiades in 313. Very little is known of him other than he is often mentioned in ecclesiastical history and later legends. He was eventually elected Pope and died in 335.

> ✟✟ *This is the Holy Cross, where our Lord died. Father Saint Sylvester, highest mountain, I beg you to free my body and my home from all wrong doing, sorcery, witches, and of sinful men and women. Free my family and myself from all enemies visible and invisible.*
>
> *In the Sacred Heart of Jesus, I ask as I put in sugar to sweeten this bath, that my future and that of my family be sweetened.*
>
> *I ask in the name of Saint Teresa, as I put Basil in the bath, to remove all the evil which may be in my home and family.*
>
> *I ask in the name of the Holy Cross that as I put in the Jerusalem Oak, as many seeds as it may have, let it be the money and abundance of health that shall come to me, my home and my family.*
>
> *I ask in the name of Saint Inez, as I carefully put in the herb called "Yerba Santa Maria", let all evil directed to my home and family be stopped.*
>
> *In the name of the Kings of Heaven, Jesus, Mary, and Joseph, I finally ask that, as I sprinkle the bath at 12:00 noon, good luck will come to me. This I ask in the name of the Lord. Amen.* ✟✟

Say one Creed, one Hail Mary, and one Our Father.

✠✠ *PRAYER TO* ✠✠
SAINT VERONICA

✠✠ *To you, divine Saint Veronica, princess of com-passion and mercy for humble hearts, I direct this plea. Gaze upon us once more, sinners that we are, who suffer in this vale of tears.*

To you, brave and compassionate Saint Veronica, who, upon seeing our Lord Jesus Christ carried to prison by the soldiers, spat upon by the heretics, and struck by the executioners, went to the Face of the Holy Teacher, soiled by dust, sweat, blood, and saliva, you crossed bravely to him, and cleansed his face with a white linen cloth and saw with amazement the face of the Nazarite reflected in three sheets of the blessed cloth. Such was your reward for your compassionate and charitable ac-tion.

Oh brave Christian, sanctified for all, we kneel before you, humbling ourselves so that you will raise the image of Our Savior to our hearts, as you raised the cloth so that no one would forget Him and we would always adore Him until the end of our lives. Amen.

By the tenderness and piety of Veronica, the blood-stained face of Christ was wiped, and as an engraved reward, the image of the Lord Sweet Redeemer remained on three sheets of cloth. In my breast His image is guarded. I lament my sins and ask for pardon. Amen. ✠✠

✝✝ *PRAYER TO THE* ✝✝
7 PSALMS OF THE HOLY SACRAMENT

✝✝ *I offer myself to the Great Power of God and the arms of the Holy Mother, the 7 Psalms and the Holy Trinity Father, Son, and Holy Spirit. I offer myself to the three cords with which soldiers tied our Lord Jesus Christ to the cross. With these same cords let my enemies be tied, from their hands to their feet. Jesus, free me from the diabolic arts. Jesus free me from all harm, and free me from evil temptations.*

I offer myself to the 7 Psalms and the 47 Angels of Heaven so that I will not be jailed nor my veins corrupted, so my enemies will not follow me with lies and gossip. Let them all come humbly to my feet as our Lord came to die at the foot of the Cross. Let them have eyes and not see me, hands that will not touch me, feet that will not reach me, and thoughts that will not be on me. Amen. ✝✝

✝✝ *PRAYER TO THE 13 RAYS OF THE SUN* ✝✝

At 1:00 o'clock the sun is higher than the moon.
At 2:00 o'clock the two slates of Moses written by our Lord Jesus Christ.
At 3:00 o'clock the three patriarchs.
At 4:00 o'clock the four wounds of our Lord.
At 5:00 o'clock I feel his love.
At 6:00 o'clock the six candles which gave light to Galilea.
At 7:00 o'clock the seven pains which the Holy Mary suffered for her son.
At 8:00 o'clock the incense will clear my mind.
At 9:00 o'clock look at yourself, my friend, and nine enemies are gone.
At 10:00 o'clock I shall guard the Ten Commandments.
At 11:00 o'clock the Eleven Thousand Virgins will be with me and will guide me safely through evil paths or danger.
At 12:00 o'clock the Twelve Apostles will accompany me along my way. Imprisoned Satan, you will not touch me from any direction.
And for the last one, I will find peace. Amen.

Make your petition, and make the sign of the Cross.

✞✞ *PRAYER TO* ✞✞
THE 7 AFRICAN POWERS

The Seven African Powers are deities of the Yoruba religion. These deities are known as orishas. Specifically they are Obatala, Yemaya, Ochun, Chango, Orula, Ogun and Elegua. Each orisha is identified with natural forces as well as with human interests or endeavors. These orishas are mediators between humanity and the Supreme Being.

> ✞✞ *Oh Seven Powers that are the Saint among Saints. I humbly kneel before your miraculous picture to ask your intercession before God, loving Father that protects all creation, living and dead, and I ask in the name of the most sacred and sweet name of Jesus, that you accede to my plea and return to me spiritual peace and material success, receeding from my house and removing from my path the dangers that are the cause of my evils without ever being able to torment me again. My heart tells me that my wish is just and if you accede to it, you will add more glory to the blessed name for years and years of our God, from whom we have received this promise. ✞✞*

✞✞ *PRAYER TO ANIMA SOLA* ✞✞

The Lonely Spirit is a representative of souls who are in purgatory. These souls are being purified in the eternal flames, waiting for a moment when they will be released from their suffering and join the souls of the elect in heaven. This spirit is used in magical works, as it will agree to work with humans in order to get their help in shortening its time in purgatory. This is allegedly possible through the giving of candles and prayers to the Lonely Spirit in exchange for its help in human affairs. **NOVEMBER 2**

✞✞ My soul, of peace and war. Soul of the sea and of the land. I want all that I have absent and lost be returned or to reappear.

Oh, Loneliest of Souls, deserted from purgatory. I accompany you in your pain. As I see you in that hard and narrow cell, I want to relieve you of your afflictions. You shall pass in this life to pay for our sins.

With your grace you shall be my benefactor. Please ask God to help me. I want to understand what is necessary for me to obey the Holy Laws. I shall love God over my neighbors and even myself. This is the way I shall find mercy and salvation forever. Amen. ✞✞

Say five Our Fathers, Hail Mary and Glory Be.

✞✞ *THE APOSTLE'S CREED* ✞✞

✞✞ I believe in God, the Father Almighty, Creator of heaven and earth; and in Jesus Christ his only Son our Lord; who was conceived by the Holy Spirit, born of the Virgin Mary, suffered under Pontius Pilate, was crucified, died, and was buried. He descended into hell; the third day he arose again from the dead; he ascended into heaven, sitteth at the right hand of God the Father Almighty from thence he shall come to judge the living and the dead. I believe in the Holy Spirit, the holy Catholic Church, the communion of Saints, the forgiveness of sins, the resurrection of the body and life everlasting. Amen. ✞✞

✞✞ *PRAYER TO* ✞✞
BUDDHA - GOD OF HAPPINESS

✞✞ *Oh mysterious spirit that directs all of our lives, come down to my humble residence. Illuminate the way to succeed through the secrets of the lottery, the prize that will give me fortune, and with it, the happiness and the well being of my family.*

Oh great source of power and wisdom, please show me the way to see to all my needs, and do not allow my enemies to harm me.

God of the Oriental, illuminate my path with the same intensity that you illuminate the paths of true believers, and remove from my path all obstacles that have been placed there by my enemies. Amen. ✞✞

✞✞ *PRAYER OF THE DEAD* ✞✞

✞✞ *Death, you find yourself in the cemetery. I call to your spirit and say, "I need to control the thoughts of those who wish evil for me. Let them not see me. Let them not offend me with words. Death, let the wine for my body never end nor the bread to sustain my being and the blessings of thy Father to fortify my soul."*

I have seen the Intranquil Spirits and those who do harm unto me.

Virgin Mary, mother of Jesus Christ, help me in the danger I face. The tears you have shed for your son, let them be the blood of my body so that all the witches and sorcerers do not kill me or see me. Let the crown of thorns that was put on Jesus be the cloth that covers my enemies. Let the chains of Saint Blas be my defense and the sword of Saint Michael conquer my enemies. I throw one of the nails which was used by Jesus into the sea, and let the waves wash over it to destroy all evil thoughts against me. Amen. ✞✞

61

✞✞ *PRAYER TO* ✞✞
THE CONGO SPIRIT

✞✞ Oh, glorious black spirit, for your virtues you have reached the Holy Blessings of God, and have come to the heavenly court to be surrounded by Angels and Archangels.

I, an admirer of your strength, knowledge and great kindness, ask in the name of God, that you fill my body with your invisible powers to separate from me the evil thoughts that my enemies may want to send me.

Free me, my Congo from all evil spirits. Tie their feet, hands, and all evil thoughts.

Oh, great Congo Spirit, with your help I will defeat my enemies. With your strength I will protect myself. With your invisible powers I will be blessed with the holy power God has given you. You, oh great Congo will help me in all my needs.

I ask, oh Congo Spirit, divine protector that you guard the surroundings of my home against envy, jealousy, and bad faith. Free me, my Congo of all bad influences and do not abandon me.

I burn this perfumed candle so that you may perfume my body, home, and belongings. Amen. ✞✞

✞✞ PRAYER TO ✞✞
THE SPIRIT OF DESPERATION

✞✞ In the hour of grief of my soul, oppressed with uncertainty, I invoke with all the strength and good will of my spirit, that you possess the five senses of_____ , and let him dedicate his faith, love, and faithfulness only to me.

Come, Spirit of Desperation, hear my plea which I implore in the name of the Father, Son, and Holy Spirit. Amen.

(It is recommended that you make an oil lamp and use Life Everlasting oil.)

Christ reigns, Christ overcomes, Christ defends us from all harm.

_____ you are dominated by the powers of Saint John, dominated by the sword of Archangel Saint Michael, tormented by the lone soul so that your evil thoughts shall not reach me. Amen. ✞✞

Say three Creeds to our Lord Jesus Christ.

✞✞ PRAYER TO ✞✞
THE DOMINATING SPIRIT

✞✞ Dominating Spirit, you who dominate all the hearts, dominate the heart of _____ with the power that Saint Martha had when she conquered the Dragon. In this way I want you to dominate

Dominating Spirit, with the power God has given you, let _____ be dominated in body and soul. Let him not look at anyone except me. Let his love and affection be only for me, so that my presence will be attractive to him, and no other shall be attractive in his eyes.

Dominating Spirit, dominate my enemies with your divine power which God has given you. Amen. ✞✞

✝✝ *PRAYER TO* ✝✝
DOMINATE AN OCCULT ENEMY

✝✝ With one I recognize you. With two I see you. With three I tie you. Your blood spills, and your heart I break.

Christ reigns, Christ overcomes, Christ defends us from all harm.

_____ you are dominated by the powers of Saint John, dominated by the sword of Archangel Saint Michael, tormented by the lone soul so that your evil thoughts shall not reach me. Amen. ✝✝

Say three Creeds to our Lord Jesus Christ.

✝✝ *PRAYER OF THE DOOR* ✝✝

✝✝ Divine Providence, you who were the author of all that I believe, without whose will nothing is moved, I think of you in my moments of uncertainty so that you will guide me and protect me from evil and envious spirits.

Guide me my spirit, if any of my enemies raise their hands to hurt me or says something to harm me, turn aside their hands and their evil thoughts, and have them ask my pardon. And I will forgive them and beg God for their salvation. Guardian Angel, do not let me become a victim or be blamed for sins I have not committed for the satisfaction my enemies want from experimenting with false and obscure spirits.

In the name of the All Powerful God, I beg my Guardian Angel and the spirits that protect me that I be freed from all bad influences and temptations and that those false and seductive spirits will not enter my body or my house and that the spirits of light will save me forever. Amen. ✝✝

✞✞ PRAYER TO ✞✞
MAKE A FORTUNE

✞✞ In the name of our Lord Jesus Christ, Father, Son, and Holy Spirit, I invoke you, Benificent Spirit, to be my help, my support, and protector of body and soul. Increase my riches, be my treasure for the virtue of the Holy Cross of Passion. I need you and all the Angels of the heavenly court. For the suffering of the blessed Virgin Mary, and for the Lord of the army which shall judge the living and the dead.

To you, who are the beginning and the end, King of Kings, Savior, Lord, and my God to whom all the saints invoke, I bless you for your precious blood which you gave to save sinners. I ask you to join in the celebration of my faith. Amen. ✞✞

✞✞ PRAYER TO ✞✞
THE MARVELOUS GARLIC

✞✞ Miraculous Garlic, you who were put in the Mountain of Calvary where Jesus died, to give eternal light and free us from all evil, free me from jail and demons. When my enemies intend to kill or hurt me, let their eyes not see me, and their feet not reach me.

Do not let their hands touch me nor their guns shoot me. Let their knives miss me, and let no harm come to me.

Miraculous Garlic of goodness, eliminate all envy. Separate me from the enemy. Help me in my work or business. Assure me the love of those around me. That is how it should be. So be it. Amen. ✞✞

65

✝✝ *PRAYER TO* ✝✝
THE SPIRIT OF GOOD LUCK

✝✝ Oh, Mysterious Spirit that directs all the course in my life. Descend onto my humble home, illuminate me through the confused Secrets of the lottery, the prize that my heart will receive, observe my intentions that are pure and good hearted and are directed in a manner to do good and help me and all human beings in general.

I am not ambitious for riches, so that I can be egotistical and a show off, I only want the money to buy the peace of my heart, help the ones I love and to better the stock in myself.

Oh, Powerful Spirit, if you think that I should still pass many days on this earth, suffering the inconveniences that destiny sets forth to me, do what you will; I resign myself to your wishes, but have in mind my good purposes which I have in mind at this moment in which I invoke the necessity in which I find myself, and if it is written in the book of my destiny, be they satisfactorily attended to; my vows which are expressed with all sincerity from my heart. Amen. ✝✝

✝✝ *PRAYER OF THE GOOD PATH* ✝✝

✝✝ I invoke the sublime influence of the Eternal Father to obtain success in all the affairs of my life and to level all the difficulties which are in my path.

I invoke the help of the Holy Spirit so the good stars will light my path and scare away the evil shadow which follows me.

I invoke the name of God so that my home will prosper and my purpose and person will receive the message of good luck sent by the Divine Providence. Oh, Great Hidden Power, I implore your supreme Majesty to keep me away from danger and let my path be illuminated by the Beacon of Good Fortune. ✝✝

66

✟✟ PRAYER TO ✟✟
WIN THE LOTTERY

Say this prayer devotedly before you go to bed. After that, you should place it under your pillow.

✟✟ Mysterious Spirit, direct all the threads of my life. Descend upon my humble residence. Guide me to find, by way of the secret chance of the lottery the prize which will bring me fortune, good-will and rest. Penetrate my soul and examine it. See that my intentions are pure and noble. That they go forward for my good and that of humanity in general. I do not want the riches only to be selfish. I desire the money for the peace of my soul, the virtue of my loved ones and the prosperity of my enterprise. Amen. ✟✟

✟✟ MONEY DRAWING ✟✟

✟✟ With the help of God, I will always have anything I need. I have my wallet blessed by God, open, not only to receive, but also to give to the needy. Permit me to use this money wisely. There should be no road closed to me.

If I should need something, please God, show me the way to obtain it. I have faith.

Oh Lord, You who have the power to give, help me resolve my problems, and let me have enough money and health to satisfy me.   Amen. ✟✟

✟✟ OUR FATHER ✟✟

✟✟ Our Father who art in Heaven, hallowed be thy name, thy Kingdom come, thy will be done, on earth as it is in Heaven.

Give us this day our daily bread, and forgive us our trespasses, as we forgive those who trespass against us, and lead us not into temptation, but deliver us from evil. Amen. ✟✟

✝✝ *PRAYER OF THE NEEDY* ✝✝

✝✝ All powerful Lord, and Supreme maker of the Universe, forgive this mortal if in ignorance he has sinned. You who see all, hear all, and appreciate with your infinite knowledge. Look at the necessities in which I find myself and help me to get the daily bread by way of work or any means which will not weigh on my conscience.

Hear my plea Lord, which comes from my heart with the desire to fulfill theirs with me. Help me to obtain money which I need to care for my family, and help me to fulfill the ideas which I have, not only for my good, but for the good of mankind.

Give me strength so that I may continue to fight these tests which burden my body and impair my spirit.

Not for my pride Lord, but so my mission may be more passable and that I may tolerate the jealousy and discord of those who surround me, to continue, without doing anything to affect my personal integrity or harm my present existence nor move back in the future.

Thanks I give you Lord, for your infinite goodness because of your mercy, I cannot doubt that you will help me to make my ideas come true or to find work which I need. Amen. ✝✝

✝✝ *PRAYER FOR PEACE* ✝✝

✝✝ Lord, make me an instrument of your peace.
Where there is hatred, let me sow love;
Where there is injury, pardon;
Where there is doubt, faith;
Where there is despair, hope;
Where there is darkness, light;
Where there is sadness, joy.
Oh Divine Master, grant that I may not so much seek to be consoled, as to console;
To be understood, as to understand;
To be loved, as to love;
For it is in giving that we receive;
It is in pardoning that we are pardoned;
And it is in dying that we are born to eternal life. ✝✝

✝✝ PRAYER FOR ✝✝
PEACE IN THE HOME

✝✝ Peace, Lord, I am one of the mortals who some- times walks blindly down my road. By succeeding, I will be able to lead and not follow. But all is hopeful because of your greatness. I want peace as much as I want bread in my home, as the peace of the poor, of the tyrants and enemies, that shines in our minds and groups us together, comes from the same fountain, so that with our spirits resolved in peace, we can be transported to the world of the beautiful.

Oh sacred peace that flies from our hearts as the dollar flies from our pockets, do not abandon us; we know that the spirit of God is the spirit of peace.

Cover us with the veil of your grace and your own magnificence. Glory to God in the highest and peace among men of good will. Amen. ✝✝

✝✝ PRAYER TO ✝✝
THE RUE FOR MONEY

✝✝ Rue, green and perfumed wherever you are placed you bring luck.

Your secret is as no other and never shall you be in need. There is no other in comparison, You free us from all harm and bring good fortune.

For this reason I await your help, sprinkling your water at my door, for as it is opened, love and money shall enter. Amen. ✝✝

✝✝ PRAYER OF THE RUE ✝✝

✝✝ Holy Rue, powerful and miraculous Rue, for the tears that were shed by the Virgin, bring to me my darling _____ .

I do this bath, bring me luck and the man I love. Let him feel love and desperation for me. Have his eyes and thoughts only on me.

For the drops of blood the King of Kings bled, I ask that you pour money and the attentions of my fellow man especially _____ .

Bring me prosperity and luck in the moment I bathe with this water. Let luck and prosperity pour over me.

This is why I ask, Holy Rue, that you give me riches, and I beg you to let happiness enter my body and soul.

✝✝ PRAYER TO THE FIVE SENSES ✝✝

✝✝ Almighty God, Merciful Father, Radiance of Light, Supreme Justice, Salt of Salts five different names for only one power. God and Nature, meaning the same, "and the Five Products of Him, the man with Five Senses to discover life with the miracle of the Cross. The Holy wood which Christ carried on his back to free us from all sin and evil.

These are the Five Senses that I want to dominate in the present and in the future, so when I see him, He will see me. When I hear him, He shall hear me. When I look at him, He will look at me. When I touch him, He will touch me, and when I sigh, He will sigh also. In this way my Five Senses will be attached to God in one thought, and I will have my way. Amen. ✝✝

Say one Our Father.

70

✠✠ THE SACRED HEART AND THE WORLD ✠✠
A CONSECRATION

✠✠ Most sweet Jesus, Redeemer of the human race, lookdown upon us, humbly prostrate before your altar. We are yours and yours we wish to be; but to be more surely united with you, behold each one of us freely consecrates himself today to your most Sacred Heart. Many indeed have never known you; many, too, despising your precepts, have rejected you. Have mercy on them all, most merciful Jesus, and draw them to your Sacred Heart. Be King, Oh Lord, not only of the faithful who have never forsaken you, but also of the prodigal children who have abandoned you; grant that they may all return to their Father's house, lest they die of wretchedness and hunger. Be King of those who are deceived by erroneous opinions or whom discord keeps aloof, and call them back to the harbor of truth and unity of faith, so that soon there may be but one flock and one shepherd. Grant Oh Lord, to your Church assurance of freedom and immunity from harm; give peace and order to all nations, and make the earth resound from pole to pole with one cry: Praise to the Divine Heart that wrought our salvation; to Jesus be glory and honor forever. Amen. ✠✠

✠✠ 23rd PSALM ✠✠

✠✠ The Lord is my shepherd; I shall not want. He maketh me to lie down in green pastures. He restoreth my soul. He leadeth me in the paths of righteousness for his names sake. Yea, though I walk through the Valley of the Shadow of Death, I will fear no evil. For thou art with me. Thy rod and thy staff they comfort me. Thou prepareth a table before me in the presence of my enemies. Thou anointeth my head with oil. My cup runneth over. Surely goodness and mercy shall follow me all the days of my life, and I will dwell in the house of the Lord forever. Amen. ✠✠

✝✝ *PRAYER FOR THE SICK* ✝✝

✝✝ *My God, your views are impenetrable and in Your wisdom You permit the affliction to _____ with this sickness. I implore you to take a compassionate look over his sufferings and dignify yourself to put an end to it.*

Good spirits, ministers of the Almighty, I pray for you to second my wish to alleviate him; make my prayer go and pour a healthy balsam on his body and let it be consoling for his soul.

Inspire him to patience and submission to the will of God, give him strength to spend his pains with resignation, like a Christian, so that he should not get weak and loose the benefit of this test to which he has been submitted. Amen. ✝✝

✝✝ *SPIRIT OF HATE* ✝✝

✝✝ *Holy Spirit of Hate, hear my pleas in this moment of disgrace.*

I desire that you inspire in me eternal hate against _____ so they will never remember _____ and for the rest of my life disappear from my presence.

Oh Holy Spirit let my heart come alive with mortal hate. As hate existed between Artaro and Belcebu, so the presence of my enemy is repulsive to me. ✝✝

This prayer should be said with a picture of Saint Caralampio, followed by five Our Fathers and five Hail Mary.

✝✝ *PRAYER FOR THE SOLDIERS* ✝✝

✝✝ Oh my God, permit that a ray of light shine in the minds of the great rulers of the nations of the world. Oh my God, permit the peace to benefit all. Oh Jesus of Nazareth, enlighten the minds of those men responsible to make a just and reasonable peace. Let the black clouds which wrap those minds be dissolved. My God, penetrate the light of reason with good understanding of the peace we all desire. My God, let our soldiers return to their homes safe and sound.

Oh Heavenly Father, make your justice for all human beings. Have all the mothers of the universe make a just petition to your immense power. You who can do all, and who are the Supreme Maker of all creation, we desire to be heard in this plea. My God, so we may devote ourselves in the obligation which we were laid by the master Jesus of Nazareth. May we love each other, so the light will shine again in the reasoning of our souls.

Ahead Soldiers, ahead God always understands and helps those who do not desire to kill, but by the law of destiny have to go to war. May the Guardian Angel protect them in all the hours of the day and night, and that soon, my God, we will all be happy in complete harmony. Amen. ✝✝

All mothers, wives and families should say this prayer. It is an obligation.

✝✝ *PRAYER TO THE WANDERING JEW* ✝✝

✝✝ Oh, Wandering Jew of lovers. As you entered the temple of Jerusalem and blew out the candles of the Holy Alter, thus I want you to enter the heart of and do not let him eat, nor sleep, nor have peace until he comes to me, giving himself with all his heart, body and soul to me.

Wandering Jew, do not allow him to sit in a chair, nor lie in a bed, nor stand anywhere without hearing my voice and seeing my shadow. As church bells go on ringing, let the ringing of the heart of _____ be for me. ✝✝

✝✝ PRAYER TO ✝✝
THE 7 INTRANQUIL SPIRITS

✝✝ Oh, 7 Intranquil Spirits, Suggestive and Dominating Spirit, you who are in the inferno and cannot enter Heaven because of your ties with Satan. Grant me what I ask. For the 21 lamps that I offer this wish.

You, who nobody calls, nobody loves, I need you. I love and call you. Hear me, hear me good. I await for you to possess the five senses of _____ that you make him intranquil and dominate him. Do not allow him to be peaceful. Do not let him sit in a chair. Do not let him eat. Do not let him sleep with anyone else. Let him run, and let nobody help him I until he comes to ask for my forgiveness at my feet.

You have not as yet come to me, but you must come because the 7 Intranquil Spirits, Suggestive and Dominating will bring you, because that is the way I want it. Oh, 7 Intranquil Spirits, suggestive and Dominating, go wherever _____ is and make him intranquil in such a way that wherever he is, he will have to come to wherever I am before the 2I days and stay with me.

_____ I conjure and promise that you will be desperate as the water in the sea, and you will have to come to me, and walk after me like a dog after its master. The living after the cross and the dead after the light.

Oh, 7 Intranquil Spirits, Suggestive and Dominating, bring me _____ .

(Here you stamp your foot on the floor three times and say " _____ come to me.") ✝✝

Pray five Our Fathers and five Hail Mary,
and do not say Amen.

74

✝✝ *HOLY CROSS OF TENERIFE* ✝✝

✝✝ *Embrace me with God the Father, embrace me with God the Son, embrace me with God the Holy Spirit. May the cross of Jerusalem be before me. Bring all my enemies before my feet. Let my Father be the Lord, Saint Peter, Saint John Baptist, and Santiago be my god parents, so you may guard all the surroundings of my home and all that may be my obligation. Holy Mary, in the company of your precious Mother, be my godmother so my body may be guarded against danger. Amen, Jesus, Mary, and Joseph. Saint Elena and Saint Martha, Lone Soul and the Nine Holy Souls of Purgatory free me from evil thoughts and evil people.*

Saint John Nepomuceno, I invoke you to crush the tongue of those who wish me harm. Saint Rafael Archangel, I beg you to give me health. Saint Francis of Paul, my Lady of Charity, Saint Anthony and the Savior of the World, let these be the ones to guard me where ever I go. Let no one have evil thoughts about me. Amen, Jesus, Mary, and Joseph. Let no one stand in my way to success and help me to be victorious in all that I do. Amen. ✝✝

✝✝ *PRAYER TO THE INTRANQUIL SPIRIT* ✝✝

✝✝ *Oh, Intranquil Spirit, you that in hell are wandering and will never reach Heaven, hear me, hear me.*

Nobody calls you. I call you. Nobody wants you. I want you. Nobody needs you. I need you. Listen to me. Listen to me. I want you to get the five senses of
and you should not let him rest in peace, either seated, standing or sleeping. That he should find himself as desperate as the waters of the seas. That he should run until he humbly falls at my feet because nobody would help him. Neither a divorcee or a married woman or a widow should love him.

_____ I conjure you before this cross and God, that you are to run after me as the living after the cross and the dead after the light. Amen. ✝✝

✝✝ *TOBACCO PRAYER* ✝✝

✝✝ I offer this prayer to the Charitable Spirits for the Guardian Angel of _____ , for the Saint Day in which he was born, for the four winds, each of them and their places in which they find _____ .
Have him cling to me, love me, and do not let him forget me.

Spirit of the forces, so you can give strength to _____ , so he can love me and come to me wherever I am. Spirit of the illusions, the illusion of _____ be passed on to me. Spirit of despair so that the desperation of _____ be passed on to me. Spirit of splendor and money so that the money he brings home, will be put into my hands.

Charitable Spirits, here I surrender body, soul, and will of _____ .

Do not let him sleep, drink, walk, or work without the thoughts put into me, that my name is _____ . Amen. ✝✝

When you offer this prayer, concentrate, and smoke a cigar or cigarette, and anoint yourself with Follow Up Cologne.

✝✝ *SPIRIT OF VICTORY* ✝✝

✝✝ Direct me Lord, show me your power. Give me what I beg of you, by way of the Glorious Angel of Victory. Guide me through good paths, guide me through a straight path so that I may be able to adore the One who can do all. Give me health and strength to adore the Almighty and teach me to respond to your graces and bless your name.

Grant me, as you did your faithful followers, the perseverance for virtue and the comfort and relief from all my afflictions and illnesses. Amen. ✝✝

Say one Our Father.

✝✝ PRAYER TO THE 4 WINDS ✝✝

(To be said Wednesday to Friday)

✝✝ Soul of the 4 winds, white horse, black horse, the great power of Jude.

Jesus Christ, you came to earth with your infinite power, you dominated Saint Marcos and conquered all difficulties. I ask you to help me conquer all my difficulties.

Glorious Saint Tobias, for the passion of the Lord, for the tears Mary shed, grant me this miracle within forty days.

Victorious Rue, poisonous serpent, with the echo of your voice and of the sea, send away all my enemies, and let good luck come my way.

Say three Our Fathers and three Hail Mary, and before the ninth Friday, your wish shall be granted. ✝✝

✝✝ PRAYER TO ✝✝
THE ELEVEN THOUSAND VIRGINS

✝✝ Holy Mother, Immaculate Light, and the Eleven Thousand Virgins. I _____ stand before your throne confused by my many and grave sins with a great pain in my heart. I detest all my sins because with them I offend your Holy Son, God and my kind Lord which I love above all things. I have resolved to die before offending you again. Because I, My Lady and kind Mother, give you my all. Giving and dedicating to you as a servant and your son, now and forever and all eternity. I give you humble thanks for all the benefits which I have received and for the evil and dangers which I have been freed from with your mercy and that of the Eleven Thousand Virgins which accompany you.

My Lady, make all my thoughts, words, and ideas be successful and my life be always directed by God, to his great glory, and to your honor, and for the good of my soul. Amen. ✝✝

✝✝ *PRAYER TO THE WORKER* ✝✝

✝✝ Jesus, Mary and Joseph, when I get up, I ask for work, health, and progress. Joseph, working man, come with me when I go to obtain my bread with the sweat of my brow. The three Angels of Jesus come with me, and talk for me when I go to solicit. Saint Joaquin, Saint Peter, Saint Michael, I ask also and the seven Creeds that I pray to, help me through Jesus, Mary, and Joseph.

Oh, my God, give me bread if you think I am deserving. If not, it will be your will that decides my luck. Pardon me for my ignorances in having failed your laws. Amen. ✝✝

✝✝ *PRAYER TO YEMAYA* ✝✝
Goddess of the Sea

✝✝ Oh, Holy, Sweet Virgin Mary, Mother of God, daughter of the Supreme King, and Lady of the Angels, Mother of the Creator of all, Queen of all mercy and immense pity. As in the days of old when everyone in times of need or devotion went to your temples, you showed your love and power in many ways.

Sailors in great storms invoke you as the Lady of Reina, and thereby free themselves of the fear and the perils of the sea. In dangerous navigations offerings are made to your sanctuary at Reina, and desired ports are reached.

Those being sought by their enemies also save themselves with this your image.

The sick find themselves healed by you. All limbs, broken or weak, gain back their natural form and strength.

Bring health and strength to those who seek to be worthy of you. We hope, Dear Lady, that through your intercession, we receive what we ask for in prayer. Although we know that, because of our faults, we do not deserve what we ask for, we beg you nevertheless to answer our prayers. Amen. ✝✝

✝✝ PRAYER FOR ✝✝
ALL OF THE DAYS

✝✝ *God of infinite goodness and mercy; Almighty Lord. We beseech you, by your grace, assist our Guardian Angels and remove evil influences so that we can concentrate on the bottom of our souls and elevate our faults. We ask with fervor for that which is most suitable for all of the human race so that with our children we will feel the desire to embrace each other with an arm of brotherly affection.*

Few are our merits, Lord. We are undeserving of your consideration, and we do not deserve your Justice, but confiding in your paternal love, we hope that you will grant to us your grace so that we get what we deserve.

We pray that you grant us conformity in our proofs, relief in our difficult times, resignation in our misfortunes, patience in our sufferings, forgetfulness of our insults, deliverance from all evil passions and harmful influences, compassion for our enemies, consolation in our afflictions, prudence in our acts, the divine light of truth which illuminates the path that leads to supreme happiness, guided by the hand of our Guardian Angel who watches over us and helps us send our esteem to you.

We ask relief and spiritual guidance for our fathers, brothers, friends, and enemies, health for the sick, light for those souls in darkness of whom we are surrounded, compassion for those who are misguided, mercy for the souls that suffer neglect by men yet still seek our prayers, indulgence for those who wail in the jails and prisons, and pardon for our persecutors. Amen. ✝✝

✞✞ *PRAYER TO* ✞✞
THE SPIRIT OF THE DESPERATE

✞✞ In this hour of bitterness for my soul, oppressed by uncertainty, I invoke you, with all the strength and will of my spirit, so that you can possess the five senses of _____ . *Submit him/her to my will, and let him/her be faithful, devoted, and love only me.*

Come, Spirit of the Desperate. I ask that you hear this prayer in the name of the Father, Son, and Holy Ghost. Amen. ✞✞

It is recommended that you use Life Everlasting oil which contains the Life Everlasting flower.

✞✞ *PRAYER TO* ✞✞
THE PEOPLE OF BAD TEMPERAMENT

✞✞ Oh Spirit who acts in the body of our brother _____ . *Hear the voice that calls you to observe the obligation to God to do good and never evil. In the name of Almighty God, put the cross on your forehead as an armor of salvation so that we do not fall into temptation, selfishness, passion, or become destitute. Do you know who it is that calls to you? God, with his divine echo, wants to rebound in your soul, your lack of faith must end. Spirit of Jesus incarnate, cover us with your divine grace and let our Guardian Angel defend and guide our steps on the good path. Amen. ✞✞*

Our Father, etc.

✝✝ *THE CROSS OF CARAVACA* ✝✝
The Wishing Cross for Good Luck,
Health and Protection Against Evil

The Cross of Caravaca should be carried. It could also be framed and placed in any room in your home or nailed to the door on the inside. In case of sickness, place it on the affected part of your body, and kiss it after removing it.

Indulgences are gained in all occasions in which the Cross is used thus, pray 3 Glory Be, to the Passion of Jesus Christ, 3 Hail Marys to the Holy Virgin, and one Our Father to Saint Benito.

These prayers should be said each day when necessary in order to obtain more abundantly the fruit of your devotion.

These instructions have been extracted from the 2nd book of the Life of Saint Benito, written by Saint Gregory, Pope and Confessor.

Saying these prayers before this Cross, revealed the Vision of Saint Benito to Saint Gertrude.

They will also help at the hour of death to powerfully oppose all attacks of the internal power of the enemy to those who devoutly have prayed during their life.

And it is generally known that Pope Clement XVI always granted full indulgence to all the sinners who would say these wonderful prayers. Amen.

Say your request. Make the sign of the Cross.

✝✝ *PRAYER TO* ✝✝
THE HOLY SHIRT (SHROUD)

✝✝ *Holy Company of God, cover me and defend me from danger with the shawl of Saint Mary his Mother. Hail Mary "gratia plena dominus tecum" free me of all evil spirits. Christ conquers, Christ reigns, Christ will defend me from evil and danger. He who is Just and Lord, only son of Saint Mary, He who was born in Bethlehem on that solemn day, He who died for my sins; those who want to harm me shall not see me, their hands shall not reach me, their weapons shall not harm me, their rope shall not bind me.*

God said those who address me with this prayer shall not become ill. I will defend you although you do not ask.

"Dominus tecum." Three Our Fathers to the death and suffering of our Lord Jesus Christ, who triumphed over death and sprinkled the world with his holy water, blessing it. My Lady, soften the hearts of my opponents whose eyes cannot see me, whose feet shall not reach me, whose hands shall not touch me. With the sword of Saint Julian be victorious, with the milk of the Virgin let sprinkle in the Holy Sepulchre. Amen.

Jesus, Mary, and Joseph.

Lawrence, detain the hearts of my enemies so that I may speak to them; Jesus Christ put yourself in my place and speak for me; Jesus Christ relieve me of this worry forever. Amen. This is the prayer of the Holy Shirt (Shroud). The son of God lives; I ask His help against my enemies so that their feet shall not reach me, their weapons shall not harm me, their rope shall not bind me. By the three crowns of the patriarch Abraham, to whom I personally offer this prayer may my enemies come humbly to me Just as Jesus Christ went to the wooden cross. Blessed Saint Idelfonso, confessor of our Lord Jesus Christ, bless the host and the chalice on the altar, bless my bed, my body, my house, and all that surrounds it; free me from sorcerers, witchcraft, and from men and women with evil intentions.

Jesus, Mary, and Joseph. ✝✝

✝✝ *PRAYER OF* ✝✝
THE OPEN ROAD

✝✝ Guardian Angel, my protector, you who has the mission which my Lord Jesus Christ gave to you, and the power to guide my steps and watch over me day and night I implore you to be my guide over these roads and protect and defend me from the evil thoughts, envy, greed, and witchcraft of my enemies.

And if any shadow or evil spirit follows me on the road, with your power keep him from me. And if an enemy, at some time or other wants to harm me, I ask that you prevent his actions and remove these evil thoughts from his mind so that I do not become harmed.

Jesus on the Cross, you who descended from heaven and the earth, by God our Father you were chosen, His only Son, He gave to you the power to open my roads. Every moment I feel that the doors of my roads are being closed, and I need your infinite goodness to open these doors to bring me luck, health, and prosperity.

Christ, you are my refuge and protector. I have faith in you as if you were the Father, you who helps me and opens the path to my happiness.

Father of refuge, grant me this day the bread of every day so that I may sustain myself add my family.

I pray that my Guardian Angel will always be my guide wherever he finds me, and that the light of divine protection will always open my roads. Amen. ✝✝

Three Our Fathers and Three Hail Mary.

✝✝ *PRAYER TO* ✝✝
THE SERVANT OF GOD,
DR. JOSEPH GREGORY HERNANDEZ

✝✝ Oh my Lord God we welcome all that you do and say through our loved servant Joseph Gregory to whom, in your great mercy, you gave the power to heal the ill of this world. Give him, Lord, the divine power to heal me. As a Holy Doctor let him cure my soul and body by your grace.

I ask this, my Lord God, in the name of your Son through whom we address our prayers to you saying Our Father...

Oh Holy Trinity! I believe in you, I await you, I love you with all of my heart and I ask that you fill my soul with your grace and be sure that my soul will never leave your Holy Church or your Holy Company. We speak to you through your Holy Servant Joseph Gregory. Teach all men to love all things equally, to serve faithfully, to love thy neighbor and show holy charity. By the gospel which speaks with virtue and knowledge, I adore and bless your servant and follow his example. I Ask that you assist me in all of my needs, especially in what I now ask. Speak to us Merciful Trinity, hear our Servant, grant the favor that we ask if it is for our greater glory and good for the soul. ✝✝

✝✝ PRAYER TO ✝✝
OUR LADY OF HIGHER GRACE

✝✝ Oh Mother of divine wisdom, Mother of Higher Grace! Miserable one that I am, I prostrate myself at your feet as I ask you to consider the requests of this prayer. The first promotes your high grace, great honor and glory on earth and the dominance of the Catholic faith: Eradication of heresies, peace and accord between Christians, defeat of infidels, and the return of all captive Christians. The second is the giving of your grace to those who deserve it, the repentant sinners who abhor the evilness of their deeds and who will never again offend your infinite goodness. I wait for mercy which is in your hands, Lady, and after serving you in this life, I hope to attain Joy in the hour of divine grace. In order that I can be more deserving of the mercy of God, I ask that you attend to my needs and grant me the grace which I am going to ask.

At this time gather in silence and let each one ask what he needs and afterwards say:

Thus my Mother, I piously await deliverance. But if by chance my petition was not convincing, I resign myself to your Holy will. Only give me the patience to tolerate the work and passions of this life until its end when in happiness I will see you with your son Jesus in glory. Amen. ✝✝

✝✝ INVOCATIONS ✝✝

✝✝ Jesus, Joseph, and Mary, assist me in my last hour!
Jesus, Joseph, and Mary, may you rest in peace!
Jesus, Joseph, and Mary, I give my heart and soul to you! ✝✝

All those who recite this prayer for nine consecutive days will acquire ninety days of leniency.

✝✝ PRAYER TO ✝✝
CHANGO MACHO
SPIRIT OF GOOD LUCK

✝✝ Oh Sovereign and mysterious spirit Chango who directs the destiny of our lives, watch over me. Humbly I pray that you light the way for me to obtain, through your secrets and great power as a warrior, fortune and luck in my Job, business, and gambling so that I can take care of my needs and gain a Joyful soul and peace of mind.

I kneel before your image, I admire your power, strength, and knowledge, and I ask for your benevolence. In the name of God and the Holy Ghost, protect me from all evil influences and evil thoughts and intentions of my enemies. There will be no need to retreat because you will be with me and you will help me in all of my needs.

Chango, my guide and protector, grant me _____. (Make your request.) In the name of the Father, Son, and Holy Ghost. Amen. ✝✝

It is recommended that you carry the medal with you and use the powerful Chango Macho bath.

✝✝ PRAYER TO ✝✝
THE SACRED FAMILY

✝✝ Jesus, Joseph, and Mary, you who form the divine foundation of the Christian Church, I humbly implore you on my knees, to free me from all traps and plots of my enemies, keep all slander from me, and free me of disease. For this will bring my heart closer to the Sacred Family. I will benefit from your example and I hope to deserve your blessing. Amen. ✝✝

RITUAL CANDLE BURNING

Candle burning provides symbolism that makes our prayers complete. We do not pray to candles, we pray to God. Candles serve to illuminate the path to successful prayer. There are many conditions which it is said may be neutralized or harmonized by the burning of the proper candles. You may well wonder what candles to burn in order to induce a specific vibration for a particular objective. In a sense, the selection is largely a matter of individual interpretation.

There are many schools of thought concerning the symbolism of color and its influence upon the individual. Perhaps the most popular opinion is that in regard to the usage of Astral colors. Among astrologers it is a well recognized principle that a person's actions are governed by the sign under which they were born. Each sign, in turn, is governed by certain planets and to each sign have been assigned certain gems and colors which are said to be attuned to those born under each sign. These colors are known as Astral Colors. Below we give the generally accepted list of these colors. Where one color is stronger in its influence it is indicated with CAPITAL letters. The other colors are of secondary or lesser influence, but still far more harmonious than any colors not mentioned under each sign.

Sign	Date of Birth	Astral Colors
ARIES	Mar. 21 - Apr. 19	WHITE & Rose Pink
TAURUS	Apr. 20 - May 19	RED & Lemon Yellow
GEMINI	May 20 - June 18	LIGHT BLUE & Red
CANCER	June 19 - July 23	GREEN & Russet Brown
LEO	July 24 - Aug. 22	GREEN & Red
VIRGO	Aug. 23 - Sept. 21	GOLD & Black speckled with blue dots
LIBRA	Sept 22 - Oct. 21	CRIMSON, Black, Light Blue
SCORPIO	Oct. 22 - Nov. 20	GOLDEN BROWN & Black
SAGITTARIUS	Nov. 21 - Dec. 20	GREEN, Gold & Red
CAPRICORN	Dec. 21 - Jan. 19	GARNET, Brown, silver-gray, & Black
AQUARIUS	Jan. 20 - Feb. 18	BLUE, Pink, Nile Green
PISCES	Feb. 19 - Mar. 20	PINK, White, Emerald Green, & Black

Study this list carefully and remember your most harmonious vibratory color. Astral type Candles are available in authentic Astral colors and wherever possible those incorporating at least two astral colors should be used.

VIBRATORY INFLUENCES
OF COLORS

The color of a candle (or of anything in your immediate environment) is like a "key" which unlocks a certain compartment of your subconscious mind, and of your entire being. Those who cannot actually "see" colors can nevertheless feel their vibratory effects, because *pigment* is *matter* releasing energy at a certain rate of speed, or "wavelength." That wave-length, or frequency activates, or energizes a certain part of your being as it penetrates your sight or your aura. Its impulses are transmitted to your brain along the nerve routes.

Each color carries the vibratory effects of one of the Planetary influences, and/or one of the four "elements", -- Earth, Fire, Air, or Water.

The actual symbolization of each color will be found to differ with authority, tradition, or school of thought, and in the final analysis, the only actual true authority for *you* is yourself!

However, if you are not quite sure what each color means to you, or "reminds you of," or "makes you feel like," here are some universal guidelines from the fields of psychology, art and religion, which you may or may not accept:

BLACK

This is the most controversial of all. We will try to represent both aspects of the controversy, and you must decide for yourself.

There are those who feel that black is "evil", and disparage the thought of ever burning any kind of black candle in fear that it "releases" all sorts of bad or dangerous influences. If you have been previously conditioned to this type of belief, it is probably best that you follow your own intuition about it, because it is *your* sub-conscious mind with which you are dealing in your selection.

For those with a more open atitude, who have not been so

conditioned, there is a completely different, and more scientific side of the story.

Black is the *absence* or *void* of any and all coloring, therefore it does not radiate or emit any vibration of its own or at all! As a matter of fact, being void, it is of female / negative polarity -- absorbing rather than emitting any energy. Then, as it burns, it "releases" only that which has been placed into or upon it. So, how *you* have charged it determines whether it is "good" or "evil". Always be certain to prepare the candle carefully prior to burning it, observing the ritual of cleansing and exorcism to thoroughly remove any impressions previously placed on it through manufacture and handling in the store.

Black represents the "still of the night", inertia, the deep cold and tranquil waters -- the deepest recesses of the unconscious mind. A burning black candle symbolizes "light coming out of the darkness".

Therefore, since it does not exert any interfering energies of its own, it is a fine choice for meditation purposes, and psychic development. Many like to burn a black candle when they are requesting something of a "miraculous" nature -- that is, a *joyous* outcome to a grim or impossible situation. There is hardly a better choice, or a suitable substitute in banishing rituals of the most serious type.

WHITE

White is the balanced presence of all colors in synthesis. It therefore gives off a very positive and powerful vibration. White can be used as a substitute for any color if you want is unavailable at the time. So keep well stocked with white candles for emergencies.

White traditionally symbolizes Purity, Truth, Sincerity, Virtue of all kinds and the highest Spirituality.

RED

Red is the color of Life's blood, and emits a very strong, positive vibration. The Red influence incites (or excites) Passion, whether it be for love, sex acquisition, an intense desire of any sort, courage, energy, strength, and radiant health. Red candles are often burned for protection against any psychic attack, physical harm inflicted through Black Magic performed by enemies, and to conquer fear or laziness.

PINK

Pink is a color which generates affection, self-generosity, selflessness. It is an excellent choice for matters of domestic, or "true" love, as it symbolizes Love, Honor, Togetherness, Gentleness, and Spiritual fulfillment. Pink candles may be burned for some healings, especially of the *spirit*. Vivid, deep pinks help to "break up" bad prevailing conditions of many kinds, as they certainly dispel gloom and negativity. "Hot Pink" is a color of great joy and sensual pleasure.

ORANGE

Orange is closely akin to the Sun of midsummer. It is therefore a color of great power. It symbolizes enthusiasm, fun, vitality, stimulation, adaptability, attraction, and friendship. It is burned for success, and also to draw or attract good things and friendly people.

GOLD

Gold symbolizes Universal Fraternity, great fortune, the intuitive faculties, and the "Cosmic mind". It can be burned to promote understanding, for Divinatory rituals, and to bring about Peace in a community or group. Gold candles are also used to bring fast luck insofar as financial benefits are concerned, when the obstacles seem to exist outside of your immediate control -- for instance, if you wish to attract a buyer for something, or would like to see your stock go up.

YELLOW

Yellow is the color of the Air element (which governs mental activity) and its radiations stimulate the intellect and imagination. It symbolizes Adaptiveness, Creativity, Skills, Commerce, Medicine, Diplomacy, Counselling, and *sudden changes.*

GREEN

Green is the color of the Venus planetary influence, and also of the productive meadows of the Eatrh. It therefore symbolizes Nature, and Material gain, Fertility, Abundance, Good Fortune, Cooperation, Generosity, Good Health, and Renewal.

Green candles are burned to gain money, to bring abundance of any kind, or to bring about matrimony. Also to retain or regain a youth ful appearance; to "loosen up" a skinflint; also to promote balance and harmony in any off-balance situation. Green is also used in any circumstance requiring a fresh, healthier outlook, or a repeat or renewal of a spell in order to perpetuate it, or protect it from deterioration.

BLUE

Light blue is the color of devotion and inspiration. It traditionally represents Peace and Blessings in the home, Immortality, Tranquility, and Masculine Youth or Innocence. Light blue is often used by women to keep a man "faithful", to retain a son's love in spite of a hostile influence, etc. Hence the term "true blue".

Deeper, vivid Royal blue is the color of the Jupiter planetary influence, and represents laughter and joviality, Loyalty on a communal level, successful group enterprise, and expansion. Study the effects of the Jupiter influence carefully before electing to invoke this power, as there are many misconceptions over this controversial planet. It is one power which can easily run amok if not properly used.

PURPLE

Purple is the color of Sovereignty or Royalty, Dignity, Wisdom, Idealism, Psychic manifestation, and Spirit contact. Therefore it is used when great Spiritual power is necessary.

Purple is effectively used against Black Magic, demoniac possession (to drive away evil,) to break up a "jinxed" condition, and for Spiritual or Psychic healing. It is also used to throw up a veil of Spiritual protection.

INDIGO

Candles of such a dark hue that they are closely akin to black, but actually a purplish-blue, are the color of the Saturn planetary influence, and used primarily to promote *inertia*. They are an excellent choice for deep meditation, as they tend to still the mind of any mental activity. They are popularly burned in rituals wherein you wish to halt the actions of someone -- to stop gossip, lies, undesirable competition, or to neutralize another's magic. Indigo is also used to expedite Karma, or for "repentence", leaving a clearer insight and wisdom gained by experience.

MAGENTA

This color is rarely mentioned in most candle burning books, because it is often difficult to find -- being available usually only in the dinner taper and pillar types, and available mostly in places where candles are sold primarily for their ornamental value.

Magenta is not a color of the spectrum, but actually an illusionary "oscillation," between the infra-red and ultra violet bands, vibrating at a very high frequency. It is a penetrating color, and denotes *Super Power*. This "color" is named for the Magi, and literally means "Magic Color" and symbolizes Omnipotence. It will penetrate all planes, is etheric in nature, and has the tendency to work *fast*. Magenta may be burned with other colored candles to promote speedy action, or by itself to expedite a lagging result. It is positively the best color for Spiritual Healing, Exorcisms and quick changes of a favorable nature. You must be certain that it is a clean, vibrant hue, preferably flourescent. Less vibrant shades tend to exert a decidedly Scorpio influence, which may or may not be what you want.

SILVER (or Light Gray)

This is traditionally the color of Stability and Neutrality. Candles of this color are burned to remove evil influences, or to neutralize any existing undesirable vibrations. Silver candles used with meditation help to aid the development of psychic abilities and ESP.

Metallic Silver Altar candles can be used to invoke the assistance of The Great Mother, or Goddess aspect of Deity.

BROWN

Brown is the color of the soil -- Earth, and its vibration is concentrated in the material plane. Some people like to burn brown candles in times of financial crisis, as it allegedly attracts money and financial success.

Brown Altar candles may be used on occasions, to attract the Earth Spirits, who must always be remunerated for their aid, and properly dismissed, or returned to the Earth with a special Ritual. Many will toss a penny into the hole, when they bury the drippings and remnants of the spell. Others like to place special "gifts" upon the Altar, some traditions listing a large pantheon of Spirits, and each one requiring a special gift (such as a cigar, a glass of whiskey, a flower, an ear of corn ... etc.) These gifts are buried, of course, with the remnants of the ritual.

DRESSING OF CANDLES

Before a candle may be placed upon you Altar, or lit for ritual, it **must** be properly prepared. "Dressing" a candle consists of three important steps: Cleansing and exorcising it of any previous impressions that may be embedded in it; Blessing the candle; or "Consecrating" it for Spiritual use; and finally, Anointing, or "charging" the candle with your special intentions.

This may seem like a lot of trouble, but successful ritualists woudn't dream of taking an often-handled candle from a store shelf, placing it on their Altar and lighting it without proper dressing.

SELECTING THE
PROPER PRAYER RITUAL
FOR YOUR PARTICULAR NEEDS

In a sense the selection of the proper prayer or ritual is largely a matter of individual interpretation. Perhaps the most important suggestion that can be offered is this: Words without acts will go for naught. Learn to pray consciously, vigorously, sincerely and honestly. Try to feel the force of your praying. True prayer can come only from within yourself. The following index can serve as a guide by which you may use the prayers contained within this book. Remember however that each of us have within, the ability to create our own prayers and affirmations.

Purpose	Prayer #	Your Astral Candle plus specific offeratory candle
Achieve Perfection	17	White
Affirm Your Love of God	47	Blue
Assurance of Love and Faith	56	Pink
Assurance that God Loves You	27	White
Avoid Court Action	28	Pink
Avoid All Dangers	127	White
Avoid Deceit	21,22	Red
Avoid Enemies	3	Purple
	21,22	White
Avoid Evil	24	White
	56	Yellow
Avoid Failure	14	White
Avoid Harm	54	White
Avoid Poverty	1	White
Avoid Prison	28	Pink
	82	White
Avoid Problems	1	White
Avoid Sin	57	White
Avoid Temptation	59	White
	93	White
Become Pregnant	48	White
Blessed Home	76	Red
Bring a Loved One to You	42	White
Bring Back A Husband	23	White
	112	Red
Bring Spiritual Blessing	1	White
Cleanse Body & Soul	19	Gold / Yellow
	18	Red
	74	Red
Conquer Fear	29	White
	41	Red

	Prayer #	*Your Astral Candle plus specific offeratory candle*
Control Enemies	21,22	Red
Control Another's Thoughts	35	Purple / White
Control One's Temper	54	White
Cure Illness	18	Red
	15	White
	109	White / Red
Cure Sick Animals	13	Red / White
Defeat an Enemy	67,68	Red
	69,70	Red
	58	Yellow
	89	Pink
	91	White/Purple
Deliver the Possessed	18	Red
Destroy Evil Thoughts Against You	37	Red / Green
Eliminate Envy	95	Green
End Other's Evil Habits	16	White
Eternal Happiness	49	Blue
Faith to Live Life	30	Purple / Green / Pink
Family Unity	51	Gold
Financial Success	46	Green
	84	7 Color
	87	Green
	95,99,104	Green
For a Husband	55	Pink
Find Lost Articles	2	Brown
	6	Blue
For Acceptance	73	White
For All Needs	51	Gold
For Fertility	48	White
For Good Luck	48	White
	131	Gold
For Good Weather	20	White
For Guidance & Wisdom	38	Gold
For Health	57	White
	109	Red
	15	White
For Justice	28	Pink
For Necessities	60	Green
	73	White
	77	Blue
For Purity	51	Gold
For Special Requests	2	Brown / White
For Spiritual Healing	1	White
For Strength	74	Red
	76	Red
For Tranquility	1	White
For Understanding	20	White

	Prayer #	Your Astral Candle plus specific offeratory candle
Forgiveness of Sins	74	Red
	44	White
	78	Gold
	86	White
Good Judgement	64	Blue
Good Luck	43	Red / Green
	132	Green
Guidance	60,61	Green
	75	Pink
Guidance of the Young	71	White
Help with Difficulties	33	White
Help with Despair	36	White
Help in Time of Need	33	White
	101	Red
Healthy Family	43	Red / White
Immunity to Enemies	20	White
In Times of Need	33	Red
Luck in Business	46	Green
Overcome Difficulties at Work	50	Gold
Overcome Grief	123	White
Patience	32	White
Peace	102	Blue
Peace in the Home	46	Green
	103	Blue / White
Protect from Accidents	14	White
	36	White
Protect Your Children	34	White
	38	Gold
Protection from Enemy	95	Green
Protect from Evil	67-70	Red
	125	Pink
Protect from Harm	14	White
	89	Pink
	114	Red
Protect the Home	76	Red
	24	White
	46	Green
	82	White
	89	Green
Protection	51	Gold
	65	Red
	47	Blue / White
	80	White
Read Minds	32	White
Repent for Sins	52	Green / White
Salvation	85	Red
Settle Disputes	25	Red

	Prayer #	*Your Astral Candle plus specific offeratory candle*
Special Favors	1	White
Spiritual and Bodily Health	57	White
Spiritual Peace	84	7 Colors
Sustain Hope	30	Purple / Pink / Green
Tranquility for the Dead	88	White
Victory in Battle	67-70	Red
Virtue	25	Red
	30	Purple / Pink / Green
Victory Over Trials & Tribulation	29	White
Win the Lottery	98	Green

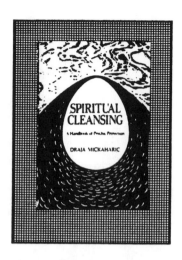

SPIRITUAL CLEANSING by Draja Mickaharic
A Handbook On Psychic Protection

This book is a manual of psychic first aid, written to help you clean your spiritual atmosphere and to protect yourself in your environment. Everyone, at some time or another, has met an individual who seems to be surrounded with negativity,or has visited a place that seems imbued with "bad vibrations". Removing these negative vibrations is what spiritual cleansing is all about. With this book you will be able to solve most of the problems of day to day negativity that may be encountered with people, places and things. It teaches how to clean away the psychic drudge in your environment, how to clean the previous tenant's vibrations out of your house or apartment, how to remove vibrations from secondhand furniture or clothing, how to cleanse your own aura. The author's "household formulas" include recipes for herb, nut and flower baths for healing, reducing tension, increasing mental acuity, bringing love into your life, or even for economic improvement. He shows how to use incense and flowers to sweeten the home and clear the air after arguments. He discusses ways of using sea salt to help invalids or children, and the efficacy of eggs to ease physical pain and for protection while asleep. These simple and effective solutions to common psychic problems are presented in a way that allows the reader to take care of his environment without spending years studying magic.
5 1/2"x8", 97 pages, paperback $6.95

THE MASTER BOOK OF CANDLE BURNING
or How to burn candles for every purpose.
by Henri Gamache

"How can I burn candles in a manner which will bring me the most satisfaction and consolation?"

In order to answer that question it is necessary to sift and sort every fact, scrutinize every detail, search for the kernel.

It is to be hoped that this volume answers that question in a manner which is satisfactory to the reader. It has been necessary, of course, to include some historical data and other anthropological data in order to better illustrate the symbolism involved in modern candle burning as practiced by so many people today.

This data has been accumulated from many sources; it has been culled from literally hundreds of books and articles. The modern rituals outlined here are based upon practices which have been described by mediums, spiritual advisors, evangelists, religious interpreters and others who should be in a position to know.

It has been the author's desire to interpret and explain the basic symbolism involved in a few typical exercises so that the reader may recognize this symbolism and proceed to develop his own symbolism in accordance with the great beauty and highest ethics of the Art.

This book is a classic, many books have imitated it, but it is the original. *The Master Book of Candle Burning* has been in print for more than 50 years. It has been read and purchased by many thousands of people all over the world. *Original Publications* has had over 50 thousand printed in the last 5 years. It is a must in the library of every person interested in magic.

5 1/2"x8 1/2", 96 pages, $4.95

♦♦♦♦♦
No desire is beyond reach,
no secret longing is unattainable,
for those who master the formulas within these pages.
♦♦♦♦♦

Money & How to Get It · Wealth & Prosperity
Gambling & Games of Chance · Jobs & Promotions
Success in Business · Wishes
Overcoming Problems

♦♦♦♦♦

$4.95

Powers of the Orishas
Santería and the
Worship of Saints
Migene González-Wippler

Santería is an Afro-Cuban religion based on an amalgamation between some of the magico-religious beliefs and practices of the Yoruba people and those of the Catholic church. In Cuba, where the Yoruba proliferated extensively, they became known as *Lucumí,* a word that means "friendship".

Santería is known in Cuba as *la religión Lucumí,* that is, the *Lucumí* religion. The original Yoruba language, interspersed with Spanish terms and corrupted through the centuries of misuse and mispronunciation, also became known as *Lucumí.* Today some of the terms used in Santería would not be recognized as Yoruba in Southwestern Nigeria, the country of origin of the Yoruba people.

Santería is a Spanish term that means a confluence of saints and their worship. These saints are in reality clever disguises for some of the Yoruba deities, known as orishas. During the slave trade, the Yoruba who were brought to Cuba were forbidden the practice of their religion by their Spanish masters. In order to continue their magical and religious observances safely the slaves opted for the identification and disguise of the orishas with some of the Catholic Saints worshipped by the Spaniards. In this manner they were able to worship their deities under the very noses of the Spaniards without danger of punishment.

Throughout the centuries the practices of the Yoruba became very popular and soon many other people of the Americas began to practice the new religion.

5¼"x8 126 pages $8.95
ISBN: 0-942272-25-0

RITUALS and SPELLS
of SANTERÍA
by Migene González-Wippler

Santería is an earth religion. That is, it is a magico-religious system that has its roots in nature and natural forces. Each orisha or saint is identified with a force of nature and with a human interest or endeavor Chango, for instance, is the god of fire, thunder and lightning, but he is also the symbol of justice and protects his followers against enemies. He also symbolizes passion and virility and is often invoked in works of seduction. Oshun, on the other hand, symbolizes river waters, love and marriage. She is essentially the archetype of joy and pleasure. Yemaya is identified with the seven seas, but is also the symbol of Motherhood and protects women in their endeavors. Elegguá symbolizes the crossroads, and is the orisha of change and destiny, the one who makes things possible or impossible. He symbolizes the balance of things. Obatalá is the father, the symbol of peace and purity. Oyá symbolizes the winds and is the owner of the cemetery, the watcher of the doorway between life and death. She is not death, but the awareness of its existence. Oggún is the patron of all metals, and protects farmers, carpenters, butchers, surgeons, mechanics, and all who work with or near metals. He also rules over accidents, which he often causes.

Many rituals and spells are included in this book, such as, To Break an Evil Spell, For Good Luck, To Attract Men, To Make a Person Return, To Make a Person Leave, these and many others to help you with all your needs.
5 1/2"x8", 134 pages, paperback $7.95
ISBN 0-942272-07-2

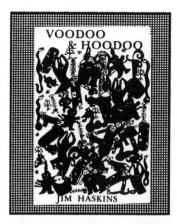

VOODOO & HOODOO by Jim Haskins
Their Traditional Crafts
Revealed by Actual Practitioners

VOODOO MEN, HOODOO WOMEN & ROOT DOCTORS,
say they know how to use eggs, graveyard dust; pins and
nails; red flannel bags; yellow homespun; urine, feces, and
blood;shoes and clothing; black cats and black hens; door-
steps; and the interior and exterior corners of houses to
conjure good and to conjure evil. Voodoo & Hoodoo tells how
these spiritual descendants of African medicine men and
sorcerers "lay tricks" and work their and explains the hold
these practices have had on magic, their believers, from the
Old World origins until today. Voodoo and its variant among
black Americans, Hoodoo, are still practiced. These are the
stories and secrets of the hoodooers, voodoo women, and
root doctors who serve paying customers all over the country right now in small southern towns and large northern
cities. Her are the "recipes" they use to attract a man or a
woman, to keep a over faithful, to avoid the law, and to win
at numbers. Here's how they use graveyard dust to cast
powerful spells, and the uses theymake of High John the
Conqueror root, Luck-in-a-Hurry Incense and many other
items, to work signs, uncross tricks and gain power over
others. A privileged survey of conjury in the American black
subculture, Voodoo & Hoodoo traces the phenomenon from
it's African roots to it's practice in Africa today.
51/2"x8", 226 pages, paperback $9.95

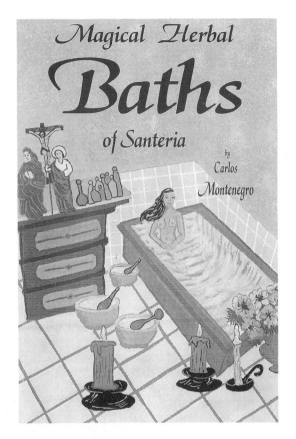

MAGICAL HERBAL BATHS OF SANTERIA
by Carlos Montenegro

One of the reasons that Santeria has become so popular is due to the use of natural remedies and herbal medicines prepared by the Santero Priests. By combining elements of spirituality with that of nature, a Santero Priest can accomplish great success with even the most difficult case. Spiritual herbal baths are widely used in the Santeria religion. Although all of the ingredients are natural, when combined with powerful supernatural magic, these herbal baths can produce incredible results. Spiritual baths have been used for hundreds of years to heal sickness and for supernatural power. The Montenegro Family has been practicing Santeria for over 200 years. This book explores the mysteries and techniques of preparing herbal baths used in traditional Santeria. The book contains lists of herbs, oils, powders, rituals and other magical ingredients used by Santeros for hundreds of years. *Orisha baths, love baths, money baths, cleansing baths, sweet baths and also baths used in Palo Mayombe and traditional Mexican witchcraft.* $5.95

Learn to Work with Natural Magic

_____ Draja Mickaharic _____

A Century
of Spells

**A collection of over one hundred
useful spells . . . that work!**
By the author of the best-selling Spiritual Cleansing

A CENTURY OF SPELLS by Draja Mickaharic

This book is a practical introduction to natural magic.It is
a work book designed to help you learn magic, and it can
serve as a practical reference for any practicing magician.
You will work with many different kinds of spells from a
number of different magical practices.This will give you an
overview of the field of natural magic so you can decide if you
want to work with the advantages and limitations of the
magical art. You will learn protection spells, and also how to
reverse spells that have been directed at you. The author
provides complete instructions for working with water spells,
baths, sprinkles, incense, oils, and herbs. He has included
some spells of Obeah and Wanga, spoken spells, and a host
of interestingspells-such as the Seven Knob Wishing Candle
Spell, Four Thieves Vinegar, Lodestone Spells, how to work
with bath salts, and how to make your own Obi stick. The
instructions are clear, and the author shares his personal
experience gained from working with these spells, so you
know they are tried and true. By the author of the best
selling "Spiritual Cleansing".
5 1/2"x8", 168 pages, paperback $8.95

protection